Unmasking the Future

exposing lying signs and wonders

Caspar McCloud

UNMASKING THE FUTURE

Caspar McCloud

© September 2016

Published by Life Application Ministries Publications (LAMP)

Cover Design: Matt McCoy

Printer: Createspace.com

INDEX

DEDICATION TO YOU

It sometimes amazes me how many people today, rather than seeking the answers in the Holy Scriptures, tend to assume such organisations as NASA have genuine answers to the complexities of the universe. After all NASA's origins clearly started by operation paperclip involved having more than 1,500 German scientists, engineers, and technicians all programmed and working for Nazi Germany to be transferred over to the United States for government employment in the aftermath of World War II. The only reliable answers we have come from our Holy Guide Book to the Supernatural—the Bible.

By studying the Word of God one shall soon come to the conclusion and discovery such things and UFO's are not travelling and appearing here from some distant planets. Rather most likely they are inner-dimensional highly deceptive spirits that manifest as disembodied demons, extraterrestrial, ghosts, space aliens, leprechaun, imps, jinn, reptilians, hybrids, and at times even appearing to look like humans.

As Tommy James quoted, "We're not alone now" is all too true. This book is for you to learn what is really going on in our world in hopes to help you prepare as we unmask the future all its deceptions, lies and innuendos. The truth makes us free, and we need to see ALL the truth about what is going on behind the scenes. This is not to bring fear but to bring discernment, and to give you a starting point—because this is just a brief look into some of the topics. So join me as we embark on an amazing wealth of discovery as we unmask the future together.

— In His Love, Caspar McCloud

ENDORSEMENTS

There are a handful of real "pastors" that I know today—I could count them on one hand. Caspar is one of them. In this book, he has done a masterful job of expressing what we are all faced with today—that of unbelief in the church and how many refuse to understand that the Supernatural continues to manifest today in ways that most people are unaware of. While much of it exists in the shadows of worldwide governmental corruption, we are now seeing real and tangible examples of what secular media refers to as the "paranormal." Because of the uncomfortable nature of these topics, many churches avoid talking about it. This includes UFOs, aliens, abductions, a One World Government, the Torah Codes, the discovery of unusual species of what can only be referred to as human hybrids in various parts of the world, and many other real and prophetic examples being revealed today.

While most churches seem to understand that the New World Order (NWO) is part of Biblical prophecy, most consider the rest as not of God, incongruent to Scripture, too "dark," and some get downright angry about it, avoiding it like the plague. And yet, these things are perhaps some of the most interesting and exciting revelations in Scripture—the very things that would bring people back into their churches—at times even physically proving these ancient texts to be more than mere myth. As Caspar points out, we are told that incredible things are indeed supposed to happen. The Scriptures tell us about the future so that when it does occur we will not be surprised. No matter how unbelievable it may seem, being suddenly caught in a state of ignorance is never preferable to being informed. The entire Bible tries to keep us in the loop of what has happened, or is about to happen.

Some say that miracles for the most part ended during the period shortly after Yeshua/Jesus left for heavenly places. After that, the world fell into centuries of cover-ups, persecutions, power struggles, deceit, false religions and messiahs, strange signs in the sky, banned passages of Scripture, and so forth. Now in our lifetimes, and much because of all our technologies, we have access to things that would have been considered forbidden knowledge only decades ago. Indeed, the circle of our own liberties, again, seem to be collapsing around us as we struggle for the truth. None of us know how much time is left. As the world devolves into chaos, our understanding of how we are to rise above such an environment has already been revealed. We need to desire more than the simple "milk of the Word" that we've heard a hundred times before. If you read this book, you're going to need to lose the baby teeth and grab a steak knife. I would encourage everyone to explore it with an open mind and heart. Caspar helps us grasp what we've been taught for decades is often based on the church's own form of "political correctness," and while that kind of philosophy is already killing our country, the church is close behind.

— Richard Shaw Director: Pinlight LLC

There are few people with the knowledge and experience of the supernatural as Caspar McCloud. I have known Caspar for years and he genuinely operates with a firm belief in the miraculous as well as a clear awareness of the malicious side of the unseen realm. Caspar's own experience of dying from a heart condition only to come back with a brand new heart is a testimony to what Caspar has been called to do. *Unmasking the Future* offers important insight into many things dismissed by most churches. The enemy wants us to remain ignorant of his devices. Don't fall for the trap. Read this book!

— Russ Breault
President, Shroud of Turin
Education Project, Inc.
www.ShroudEncounter.com

Pastor Caspar's new book will challenge the reader. Do we really believe what is in our Bibles? We read about talking donkeys, floating ax-heads, a virgin birth, coins that appear from the mouth of a fish, men that walk on water, water that is changed to wine, water that is heaped up and seas that part. Staffs are thrown to the ground and become snakes, men that are in one location and then suddenly are whisked away only to find themselves miles from where there were in an instant. The future of our planet is told with great specify. Prophecies are written sometimes thousands of years before their fulfillment. Caspar believes in the supernatural! Bully for him. There is a tension within the body of Messiah, or the Christian church. There is a division between those who take the Bible literally with all of its supernatural events and those who maintain and insist that all of this passed away with the passing of Jesus' apostles. Yet, as Caspar points out, our Bibles confirm that the supernatural will be on steroids in the last days. What do we do with scripture from our savior that warns us: Men will faint from fear what is coming upon the earth? I believe we are in the end times and Pastor Caspar's writings will equip the reader with what I believe is vital information. UFOs, the days of Noah and the return of the Nephilim, the rise of the occult. Pastor Caspar tackles these subjects with erudition. Dive in and study to show yourself approved!

— L. A. Marzulli CEO Spiral of Life
www.ppsreport.com

There is a movement within the church that has chosen to interpret end-time Scriptures allegorically. Many last days prophecies have already come to pass and more will shortly be fulfilled. The danger of this allegorical view is that as the Messiah's return draws near, some believers will miss the signs.

In his book, *Unmasking the Future*, Caspar does a masterful job explaining long-prophesied events that are converging at this very time in history. The fulfillment of these Scriptures in our day clearly shows that the Lord's Second Coming is at hand. For the most part, the prophetic significance of these events has been hidden from the general public and even many believers.

At the same time, Caspar teaches us how to walk in God's love, faith and glory in these end times. As we allow the Lord's presence to flow through us we will touch lives around us and see victories as never before. And when we are filled with God's perfect love and power there will be no room for fear.

"But concerning the times and the seasons, brethren, you have no need that I should write to you. For you yourselves know perfectly that the day of the Lord so comes as a thief in the night. For when they say, peace and safety then sudden destruction comes upon them, as labor pains upon a pregnant woman. And they shall not escape. But you, brethren, are not in darkness, so that this Day should overtake you as a thief. You are all sons of light and sons of the day. We are not of the night nor of darkness. Therefore let us not sleep, as others do, but let us watch and be sober. For those who sleep, sleep at night, and those who get drunk are drunk at night. But let us who are of the day be sober, putting on the breastplate of faith and love, and as a helmet the hope of salvation" (1 Thess. 5:18, NKJV).

— Janie DuVall Speaker Music
composer/TV producer
Former producer of Sid Roth's
It's Supernatural!

'I THINK WE'RE NOT ALONE NOW...Caspar and I became friends when he interviewed me for his internet radio show... he is one of the most fascinating people I have ever had the pleasure of talking to. He is also one of the few people I am able to have a conversation with about the subject matter in his new book *Unmasking The Future*. In addition to being a strong and devout Christian, he is also a genuinely decent human being and I am so very proud to call him my friend. I absolutely love this book!

— Tommy James Recording Artist
Author of the autobiography
Me, The Mob, and the Music
Tommy James and the Shondells

I have had such fun reading and thinking about the topics that Pastor Caspar engages in his new book, *Unmasking the Future*. Caspar is, as we say in Oklahoma, a "stitch" because at one level he is lighthearted and funny, but at another deadly serious. You have to pay attention to know which way he is leaning. And he is willing to talk about the paranormal, UFOs, giants, conspiracies, and matters of fact that tell us the world is not quite what we thought it to be. For Caspar, such "paranormal activities" are proofs that we live in a spiritual world, encounter spiritual beings (mostly malevolent), and we need to tackle them in warfare. He says, tongue in cheek, that he doesn't like to go to bed at night until he has some devil blood on his sword from the day's work! Demons beware: This former rock star guitarist, now exorcist and healer, not only knows his guitar chops but how to bust the chops of the devils that come against us. But more than being a good time, Pastor Caspar McCloud has the big heart of a pastor that is always ready to extend himself to encourage and reassure. I find spending time with him in person, over the radio when we do interviews, or when reading his books gives me a warm feeling that I am in the presence of a genuine man who loves what he does and loves people to whom he can minister. I encourage you—his prospective reader—to give your attention to this book. Read carefully the scriptures he quotes, and the insights he brings to the Word of God. His wisdom will give rise to many enjoyable thoughts and images and conclude with substance that can help you build your life on the right foundation and set for you a steady course for the future.

— S. Douglas Woodward Author
Oklahoma City

Wow... I have been mates with Caspar for almost forty years. Caspar has done it again only this time on an elevated level that I never knew existed, "THE SUPERNATURAL." He pushes the layman to dive into learning more and more about things they do not know or do not understand fully. Supernatural powers seem entirely possible and probable according to Caspar and he will showcase his knowledge and wisdom and will make you want to believe as well.

— Eliot Goldstein
Tour Assistance and Coordination for
Stadium Tours,
U2/Rolling Stones / Metallica/Ozzfests/
Bruce Springstein/Fleetwood Mac
Independent Record Producer and
Artist Management

Caspar does an amazing job of looking at the rise of demonic activity, UFOs, ghosts, goblins and spookies... He is excellent at his research.

— Trey Smith God in a Nutshell Project

Pastor McCloud's new book will stretch your faith by making it firmer in The Word and it will push the limits of our earthly minds as you gain perspective through a biblical mind set. Just as Scripture tells us to have the mind of the Messiah, this means we are to think like He thought which will allows us to do as He did. There are subjects that we find in The Bible that most are unwilling or fearful to examine yet we must be able to account for our faith. *Unmasking the Future* will help you develop a biblical view of difficult Bible questions as well as help you to understand what the Holy Spirit is saying to The Church in these end days. This is a very timely and enjoyable read for the days we are living in.

— Chief Joseph RiverWind First Nations
Ministry www.TheRiverWinds.com
Award-Winning Musician
www.TheBlessedBlend.com
Published Author "That's
What the Old Ones Say,"
Act for America National Speaker

It seems that we are living in a day when Christians insist on being protected from the message of the Bible. When confronted with information that seems to be in stark contrast to the carefully crafted biblical message they are most familiar with, most Christians simply dismiss the information. Tradition, creed, confession, and comfort have all surpassed any desire to grapple with the implications and truth of the Scriptures. For far too many believers today, Christianity has become a cultural identity and not a Holy Spirit led adventure of holy living and righteous testimony to our world. This form of pseudo-faith will not stand the tumultuous time of persecution that is spreading across the world.

Why do Christians in large measure, simply want to live their lives uncritically? By that I mean without observing our present realities against a biblical backdrop? Why are Christians for the most part content to attend their weekend church service and hear again the same old messages about the great need they have to be better husbands, wives, parents, or believers accompanied by twelve steps for making that happen? Is that really what the biblical message is all about? Or is there much more that we can know and absolutely must know for the days we live in? I believe it is the latter; and thankfully there are modern day prophets calling God's people to be those with "eyes to see and ears to hear" what our great God is saying today.

Pastor Caspar McCloud has painstakingly laid out the information every Christian must give due consideration to in his book, "*Unmasking the Future*." In ten chapters Pastor Caspar makes his case that God is preparing His people for the fulfillment of prophecy. The supernatural realm has been complete-ly removed from discussion and research among most Ameri-can churches and thus most Christians. Pastors have led the charge to eradicate what the Bible clearly and without apology presents as a normal world view.

Will you be numbered among those God wants to use? The pressing need of our time in America at least, is for the church to throw off the self-imposed shackles of soft serve vanilla ice cream theology and Bible teaching that melts rapidly when exposed to the glaring sun of examination, and put on instead the full armor of God as stated clearly in the Scriptures, so that we are able to stand firm against the strategies of our enemy who hates us with demonic passion. Please note friends that we are called to "take up the full armor of God, that you may be able to resist in the evil day and having done everything, to stand firm" (Ephesians 6:13 NASB). Forgive me for stating the obvious but we are living in evil days. Scoffers might counter that times have been evil before. My response is this: "You hypocrites! You know how to analyze the appearance of the earth and the sky, but why do you not analyze this present time?" (Luke 12:56 NASB). Friends, the supernatural realm is real and is being revealed for a great end times awakening and deception. Whether you are being awakened or deceived lies within your ability to take Pastor Caspar's book to heart and begin to prayerful consider what God is speaking to you.

— Dr. Mike Spaulding Pastor of Calvary Chapel of Lima
Radio host of The Transforming Word and Soaring Eagle
Radio
Author of Servant Leadership, and
The Ministry of Teaching

When reading Caspar's new book *"Unmasking the Future"* one word kept coming to my mind, "Relevance." How often over the last thirty years have those of us in ministry been told that we must be Relevant if we are to reach our culture for The Lord Jesus Christ. They say we must be "Relevant" in our preach-ing, teaching and the music by which we worship the Lord. Yet when a great percentage of believers and most pastors are shown what is transpiring in our culture, our churches and how these lying signs and wonders are manifesting before our collective eyes, I am told or it is insinuated that it is not "Relevant" for the church. I have personally come to the conclusion what the contemporary church has been proclaiming with a loud voice has not been Relevance but rather Compromise dressed in "The Emperor's New Clothes" of being Relevant!

Caspar's new book *"Unmasking the Future"* truly is Relevant for our time in which we find ourselves pushing back against the onslaught of preaching and teaching that is void of the truth of God's Word! We the people of God need to be informed of what the enemy of our souls is doing in his effort to deceive mankind. The Pastors of God's Church must sound the clarion call of warning while there is still time to snatch those who are spiritually standing on the edge of destruction before it is too late. The Father is about to sound the trumpet and call the Lords Body home. Until the Rapture of the Church we must stand in the power of the Crucified Christ!

In the Master's service,

— Bishop J. E. Farster, Pastor
Freedom's Light Church of God

It has been a great honour and true privilege to know Caspar as a friend and brother in Christ. He is a man after God's own heart and serves the body of Christ in ministry with pure motives, fired by His love. With so much compromise in the church world-wide today, where many preachers have become merely motivational speakers who barely teach from Scripture anymore—Caspar has a passion to share the pure, undiluted, un-compromised Word of God.

I have tremendous respect for Caspar and his boldness to educate the Church and Bride of Christ about the up-coming world changes and events that will soon take place, when many do not have the courage to speak about it and would rather avoid the subject altogether. However, there is no topic more timely and relevant than this one! The King of Kings and Lord of Lords is coming back for His Bride and to rule and reign over this entire world! How can this not be the most vitally important event in all of history? We are in exciting times! The signs are certainly there that we may be the generation that experiences the conclusion of the promise of Christ's return!

Therefore, this is essential knowledge that every true, born again, Spirit-filled Christian believer should be equipped with, so that we can understand what is unfolding in world events - in view of the Biblical prophecies which are presently being fulfilled concerning these issues. Ignorance is one of the enemy's greatest weapons. Many are completely unaware of how close we are to the edge of time. What shall happen when the Great Deception plays out on the world stage and most of our church members are clueless to what is taking place? We need to be aware of these things so we aren't caught off guard when faced to make a hard choice concerning them.

Proverbs 22:3, *"A prudent man foreseeth the evil, and hideth himself: but the simple pass on, and are punished."*

Caspar has an incredible ability to share the truth, yet with so much love and humility. Rather than opening the door to fear, he brings constant encouragement and hope about the return of our Bridegroom and King. This is what 1 Thessalonians 4:18 tells us to do: *"Wherefore comfort one another with these words."* Being able to use the Word of God to separate the truth from the lies and deceptions, makes us free of what is manifesting before us all around this fallen world today... and helps the church be relevant in this area and equipped to properly address the reality of what is talking place globally from a Biblical perspective.

The prayer of both mine and Caspar's heart for you as you read this book is that you would be drawn into a more closer, intimate relationship with our Lord Jesus/Yeshua, that as a work of the Holy Spirit you would be sanctified and purified by His Word, whilst at the same time, are ready and prepared for what is coming.

Luke 21:36, *"Watch ye therefore, and pray always, that ye may be accounted worthy to escape all these things that shall come to pass, and to stand before the Son of man."*

Dr. Michelle Strydom
Eagles Wings

FORWARD

We live in an age when American adults are four times more likely to believe in ET than in God. Now, that sounds so crazy you might think I just made it up. I wish I had. A 2012 survey by National Geographic revealed that 36% of Americans believe that UFOs exist. That's about 80 million of us. And 77% believe there is at least evidence that extraterrestrials have visited Earth. Compare those numbers with the results of a 2009 survey by the Barna Group, a Christian research firm that specializes in tracking the state of America's faith. Barna found that only 9% of Americans have a biblical world view, which they defined as believing in six basic tenets of Christian doctrine—the virgin birth, Christ's sinless life, the literal existence of Satan, and so on, all Christianity 101, as it were. But only 9% of the adults in our "Christian" nation believe in God as He's revealed Himself through His Word. Why do these numbers matter? Because the UFO phenomenon is not about science and exploration, it is a religion. Ufology offers false answers to the big questions that have haunted humanity since the beginning of time: Where did we come from? Why are we here? And what happens when we die? If that sounds far-fetched to you, then—with all due respect—you haven't been paying attention. Tens of thousands of people travel across the country every year to UFO festivals in places like Roswell, New Mexico, McMinnville, Oregon and Joshua Tree, California. Ask attendees why, and they keep coming back to find answers to those questions. Where did we come from? Why are we here? What happens when we die?

We Christians have definitive answers to those questions! Why aren't they coming to us? Because all too often, we refuse to engage with seekers who have questions about mysterious lights in the sky, or with traumatized victims of experiences they can barely describe, much less understand. It is not a coincidence that the late Harvard psychiatrist Dr. John Mack found more than three dozen points of correlation between the accounts of UFO "abductees" and victims of Satanic ritual abuse.

We're not dealing with extraterrestrials. These entities are inter-dimensional. They are spiritual. They've been here on Earth with us all along. But instead of sharing the good news with people who may be in their hour of greatest need, we often make ourselves an obstacle between them and the gospel of Jesus Christ.

The preachers of the Ancient Aliens gospel are more than happy to listen without judgment. And that's why people are more likely to believe in ET than in Yahweh. So before you dismiss any discussion of the UFO phenomenon as a waste of time for ministers of the gospel, I humbly suggest you look around at the culture and ask: Why does the church of ET have more true believers than Jesus Christ? Pastor Caspar McCloud is a man with a gentle spirit and genuine heart for the Lord. His discernment and courage in recognizing the importance of this issue and addressing it are commendable, and I am honored to call him my friend.

Derek Gilbert Host, SkyWatchTV Contributing author:
Blood on the Altar and God's Ghostbusters

SPECIAL THANKS

To my dear sister in the Lord, Linda Lange, with Life Application Ministries Publishing, who coauthored my book *"What Was I Thinking?"* and who has laboured with me in the field of ministry many long years. Thank you for helping me publish this book and encouraging me along the way!

I must also thank my faithful friend and sister in Christ Lori Colley who advised and helped me write my first book *Nothing Is Impossible*. After looking at the proof copy of Unmasking the Future, I had a check in my spirit there was more work to be done. My friend Tom Horn had shown great interest in my first draft for the book, saying I was the sort of writer he was looking for with the perspective and background needed to help get the word out. This encouraged me to complete the project. At that point I sent a copy of the proof version to Lori who is someone I know I can trust with just about anything and has worked as a professional editor. Basically, I just wanted her to proof the book once more to make certain the grammar police would not eventually be coming after me.

To my amazement, Lori called me up after reading part of the manuscript and started asking for lots of clarification. Suddenly, I realised I had written the majority of this book as if I was preaching to the Choir. I suppose in my circle of influence the last several years being "on the trail" with L. A. Marzulli and Richard Shaw somehow I started taking for granted the reader would understand these absolutely bizarre subject matters. In a way, it was similar to when my friend and mentor Phil Keaggy attempted in a teaching video to show other guitarists how to play at his level of expertise and artistry. Unless you are already able to understand how to perform at a virtuoso level it probably wouldn't make much sense as several guitarists had asked me to slow down and explain to them how to play like Keaggy does. Thankfully, the Lord has used Lori's skills in editing to bring this book to a place where you shall be able to comprehend and apply the prophetic warnings unfolding before us today.

OPENING PRAYER

"Papa God we thank You for today, for Jesus/Yeshua, and for the Holy Spirit. We thank You for eternal life and for eternal identity and inheritance in You. We are so grateful and thankful that You allow us to partner with You and that we can be joint heirs with Christ.

Thank you that we are covered by His precious shed blood and that You love us with an everlasting love that we are a chosen generation, a royal priesthood, and a blessed people. We are so grateful You have gathered us together to be with You of one accord. We are glad that we can come and meet You anywhere we are and learn a more excellent way. We are so thankful that we can have the kind of intimacy with You that a child has with their father—coming boldly, any time day or night, into Your throne room and talk to You about anything at all, sharing our heart with You whilst making our requests known to You.

We thank you that You are always full of mercy, grace, and love and that You forgive us of all our sins through the shed blood of Jesus Christ. We believe that signs and wonders (healing and miracles) will follow us as we follow after You.

Help us to watch and pray always that we may be counted worthy to escape all these things that shall come to pass on this planet. We long to stand before You one day and hear You say, "Well done good and faithful friend!"

We invite the Holy Spirit to come and teach us. Overtake us with Your presence! We desire a relationship with You in obedience to Your Word. We ask that You meet us here just where we are now.

I pray that Your almighty healing hand touches each person where there is a need. I ask that blessings of Abraham overtake us and chase us down everywhere we go, in the name of Jesus Christ of Nazareth. Amen."

Chapter One

INTRODUCTION

Some time ago I showed my friend, who is a minister associated with the Church of England and a priest for many years, videos from the Watchers series by L. A. Marzulli and Richard Shaw. As we developed our friendship and shared our beliefs with one another, and at the leading of God he decided to leave his denomination. Much of what he was taught in his church was contrary to the Bible. I have great respect for his decision. It meant leaving the so-called security of organised, corporate religion and a steady paycheck, to rely solely on the supernatural provision of the Lord.

It is written in Philippians 4:19, *"But my God shall supply all your need according to his riches in glory by Christ Jesus."*

This passage says that the Lord supplies "all" our needs. This must mean everything! This priest turned pastor began to get excited about the gifts of the Holy Spirit in healing and restoration, and that those things are for today. He heard testimonies of healing and really began to understand that all true believers are now part of the priesthood.

1 Peter 2:9 *"But ye are a chosen generation, a royal priesthood, an holy nation, a peculiar people; that ye should shew forth the praises of him who hath called you out of darkness into his marvelous light;"*

My friend is also keen on my art and music endeavors and has attended several of my concerts, outreaches, and worship services over the years. He has been most encouraging to me, even though his religious background, programming, and affiliations may at times hinder our conversation—especially the supernatural power of the first century Church and the ancient, end time prophecies. Not surprisingly, he seemed quite astounded with the information shared on the Watchers videos, even though I have been trying to tell him these things for several years.

The world may say, "seeing is believing," however, the Holy Bible gives us a different perspective. For example, 2 Corinthians 5:7 tells us that we are to walk by faith and not by sight. In fact, the Lord Jesus/Yeshua said in John 20:29, *"...Thomas, because thou hast seen me, thou hast believed: blessed are they that have not seen, and yet have believed."*

I often tell our church fellowship you must believe to receive.

Mark 11:24 *"Therefore I say unto you, Whatsoever ye desire, when ye pray, believe that ye receive them, and ye shall have them."*

As we exchanged our thoughts after the Watchers video ended, I told my minister friend that L. A. Marzulli and I had been wanting to do a conference in our area. I gave him some highlights from a recent Nephilim conference (based on the giants from Genesis 6:4) that I took part in, along with Marzulli, Russ Dizdar, Randy DeMain, and Mike McClung. Whilst showing him photographs Marzulli's book, On the Trail of The Nephilim and sharing some personal insights, I could sense he was finally opening up to some revelations from the Lord.

In fact, my minister friend was quite enthusiastic about such an event coming to our area, and immediately suggested the possibility of using his church building. We prayed together and off he went. The very next day an email arrived. My friend's enthusiasm was shot down by the slings and arrows of religious advisors who were strongly against him being involved with such a conference.

It seems you can grow a big church if you just tell the people what they want to hear instead of what they need to hear.

One of my heroes of the faith was General William Booth, who founded the Salvation Army in England in the late 1800s. Booth led many people to salvation in Christ, and also saw supernatural healing and deliverances. He must have also had a gift of prophecy, because he wrote to one of his friends and said: "I consider that the chief dangers which confront the coming century will be religion without the Holy Ghost, Christianity without Christ, forgiveness without repentance, salvation without regeneration, politics without God, and heaven without hell."

Clearly, General Booth spoke prophetically!

In his letter, my friend wrote that he had showed the videos to some Christian leaders, friends who he trusted, and after receiving their comments, wanted to share them with me. They were not positive comments, and there would be no conference at his church. My answers to him are the inspiration for this book, and in a moment I'll share these things with you. Let me first say that I prayed before responding to my friend. I thanked him for being honest and transparent, and I conveyed that I certainly understood the perspective that his team of advisors were coming from. I relayed that our goal is much the same: to help all people get serious about the things of God before it is too late. We travel this path towards holiness, just like a natural motorway or highway, but we are all at different places. Some may be able to see the final destination coming into view, while others are not as far along.

We read in Isaiah 35:8, *"And an highway shall be there, and a way, and it shall be called The way of holiness; the unclean shall not pass over it; but it shall be for those: the wayfaring men, though fools, shall not err therein."*

I felt led to share how I personally saw the Lord use my dear friend Marzulli and his associates to lead people into a much closer walk with our Lord Jesus/Yeshua, while at the same time preparing them for what is coming. Rather than bringing in a spirit of fear, Marzulli has brought great comfort helping people separate truth from the lies and deceptions. We all need to have God's perspective: putting on the mind of Christ and ridding ourselves of anything that might be hindering our relationship Jesus, who is our first love.

These are indeed very troubled times—yet also very exciting times as we may be the generation that witnesses Christ's return. Hallelujah!

We read in 1 Thessalonians 4:1618, *"For the Lord himself shall descend from heaven with a shout, with the voice of the archangel, and with the trump of God: and the dead in Christ shall rise first: Then we which are alive and remain shall be caught up together with them in the clouds, to meet the Lord in the air: and so shall we ever be with the Lord. Wherefore comfort one another with these words."*

In no way do I demean those who feel uncomfortable with the subject matters presented in this book. I assume they are sincere, doing the best they know how to do with what they have been taught about the gospel. However, we are each personally preparing ourselves for the second coming of Christ, and how we do that is between us and the Lord. It is my prayer that God will help each of us comprehend that we do not have to know everything there is to know—that's why this book is just an introduction to these topics. Instead, we can simply trust the Lord in childlike faith, not leaning on our own understanding (Proverbs 3:5).

Now, let's take a look at the objections in this letter:

Hello Brother:

Thank you again for yesterday, being with you was refreshment for my body and my spirit!

Every Friday morning after 6:30 worship, a small group of us have breakfast together. This is a very devoted group of Christian leaders. Today included two board members, a woman leader, a pastor, and a seminary student pursuing full-time ministry. I deeply value their friendship and insights. I love you so much as a brother that I need to share with you their thoughts, as I invited dialog about your/our hosting a UFO program with L.A.

Following is a brief summary of their conclusions:

1) In our very busy and complex lives, ANYTHING that is not directly glorifying Christ should not be offered at the church.

2) UFOs and related topics are very interesting, but as with MANY areas for discussion, do not directly build faith; they may actually increase fear.

3) In this world, if you or I were publicly associated with the topic it would hurt, not help, our ministry of gospel proclamation because we would be perceived as "fringe religious."

4) The Truth that sets us free is Jesus, not every bit of truth on any issue. Even knowing "truth" may take our focus off the Lord.

5) This is not from God.

6) Some even ventured, that if offered at another location, they might even attend, and that it might be helpful for leaders to attend, but not for all the folks and definitely not at church.

I thought you needed to hear, therefore, I have to conclude that we should not offer L.A. Marzulli and you here at the church.

Blessings Brother

I believe that something invisible may have influencing these individuals' thoughts. I am much more concerned about what the Lord thinks than what anyone else has to say. So my response to him, and what is written in this book, are for those who have ears to hear, eyes to see, and hearts that they can be converted.

"For this people's heart is waxed gross, and their ears are dull of hearing, and their eyes they have closed; lest at any time they should see with their eyes, and hear with their ears, and should understand with their heart, and should be converted, and I should heal them" (Matthew 13:15).

The statements in his letter, which at first seem very reasonable and almost certainly religious and pious, reflect what is unfolding in mainstream Christianity today. Please understand that doctrine is vitally important, and everything must line up with the Bible, our guide book to the supernatural. However, I believe these statements fit right into the coming great deception the Lord warned us about.

1 Timothy 4:12 *"Now the Spirit speaketh expressly, that in the latter times some shall depart from the faith, giving heed to seducing spirits, (lying) and doctrines of devils. Speaking lies in hypocrisy; having their conscience seared with a hot iron."*

This passage refers to a seared conscience. That means a spirit that has been tarnished, perverted, and changed from being God led to being human led, or worse, being demon-led. A person with a seared conscience can no longer tell right from wrong. Like proclaimed in some of the false religions today, these are people who will steal, kill, and destroy anyone who disagrees with their particular perspective. Proverbs 16:25 tells us, *"There is a way that seemeth right unto a man, but the end thereof are the ways of death."* And so, they may even do it in the name of their "god."

I pray in the name of Jesus/Yeshua that more churches would be led by the Holy Spirit and begin to fearlessly preach and teach about the cross and repentance. I pray that the doctrine of universalism, erroneously teaching that all people are "saved" no matter what they believe or what god they serve, would be exposed for the lie that it is. We read in Romans 6:23, *"For the wages of sin is death; but the gift of God is eternal life through Jesus Christ our Lord."* God hasn't changed His mind about sin.

I pray that every false doctrine, including Calvinism, which caused Europe to fall into a post-Christian condition, is revealed for its deception. The Calvinist assumes that if it is God's will for people to be saved they shall be, leaving no incentive to witness. They do not believe the Lord is the same today and forever (see Hebrews 13:8), and think miracles and healing have passed away. Au contraire, mon frère.

Calvinism overlooks Scriptures like 1 Timothy 2:4, *"Who will have all men to be saved, and to come unto the knowledge of the truth."* It also overlooks 2 Peter 3:9, *"The Lord is not slack concerning his promise, as some men count slackness; but is longsuffering to usward, not willing that any should perish, but that all should come to repentance."*

Sadly, there are those who try and make Scripture fit their theology rather than fit their theology to the Holy Scriptures. Second Peter 1:20 says, *"Knowing this first, that no prophecy of the scripture is of any private interpretation."* In other words, we all ought to be able to read the Word of God and get the same message. The Lord Jesus told us the Holy Spirit would be our helper and that He will guide us into all truth and shall teach us all things.

Chapter Two

WHAT ABOUT THESE FRINGE SUBJECTS?

Now let's address the objections in the letter I received. These are the same sort of protestations raised all around the world. Is it God's agenda that this stuff be kept "fringe" so that the Church would remain ignorant? Or is it Satan's? Keep in mind that Satan and his kingdom of invisible spirits are not bound by geography. They are at work in every corner of the world to keep us from the truth.

The Religious Leaders said:

1) In our very busy and complex lives, ANYTHING that is not directly glorifying Christ should not be offered at the church.

Personally, I could not agree more! As we read in 1 Corinthians 10:31, "Whether therefore ye eat, or drink, or whatsoever ye do, do all to the glory of God." However, does this mean churches should avoid teaching about evil, hell, and damnation so no one will be offended? Should they avoid teaching and preaching about these end time prophecies because someone might become afraid?

This same argument could be used to avoid dealing with the moral breakdown in society. What do you think? Should we simply accept changes and agendas contrary to the Word of God—or should we be about our Father's business, helping people have a relationship with Jesus so they will avoid hell and have a better life? I believe the Church should be busy exposing the deceptions that are already in place.

Statement #1 actually reminds me of the Mary and Martha story. Christians are so busy with church programs and budgeted yearly agendas they neglect the things that will last. It seems the more programs a church designs, the less the Holy Spirit can intervene. Who will sit at the feet of Jesus and learn the good part that won't be taken away? Today it is difficult to tell a Christian from an unbeliever because we have not been sharing the whole gospel and preaching and teaching about these very things.

The Lord designed us with something called "mirror neurons." Research shows most forms of imitation occur through these mirror neurons. This is what gives us mannerisms and forms how we express ourselves and how we develop accents. These are also responsible for giving us cultural norms. How much better off would we be if we followed Jesus this way! It's possible because He gave us His Holy Spirit, who speaks to our spirit, telling us when the Lord is pleased and when He is not pleased. The Lord is always a perfect gentleman, giving us the choice and ability to obey.

John 14:26 says, *"But the Comforter, [which is] the Holy Ghost, whom the Father will send in my name, he shall teach you all things, and bring all things to your remembrance, whatsoever I have said unto you."*

John 10:27 says, *"My sheep hear my voice, and I know them, and they follow me:"*

Hidden Agenda: Not so Hidden

There is an agenda in place to try and cause you to look at the wind and the waves instead of keeping your sights on the awesome almighty power of the Lord Jesus Christ. We are exhorted to understand and appropriate the truth, such as Philippians 4:13, *"I can do all things through Christ which strengtheneth me."* I believe all things includes overcoming all deceptions and walking in the supernatural (John 14:12).

Many church leaders have chosen to ignore the elephant in the room and refuse to even examine the evidence. How often do we find people expressing their opinions about a variety of subjects without actually studying the facts? Many don't search the Holy Scriptures for the proper perspective and answers. Has political correctness been so programmed into the

Church that we overlook the truth and put aside critical thinking?

We read in 2 Timothy 2:15, *"Study to shew thyself approved unto God, a workman that needeth not to be ashamed, rightly dividing the word of truth."*

Does this mean we are to simply study the Scripture and totally ignore what we are observing on the world stage? I think not! Rather we are to study and understand what is quickly approaching this world. Just as the Lord Jesus/Yeshua rebuked those He said could discern the weather that was approaching and somehow still ignore the other important factors of the day and times.

Luke 12:56 *"Ye hypocrites, ye can discern the face of the sky and of the earth; but how is it that ye do not discern this time?"*

The wise men went looking for the baby Jesus because they understood that the Messiah was to be born in their lifetime. Perhaps He will return in our lifetime! We must see to it that we remain Spirit-led every moment of each day, displaying a life of service, sharing Christ's love, and watching for His return.

Luke 26:31 *"Watch ye therefore, and pray always, that ye may be accounted worthy to escape all these things that shall come to pass, and to stand before the Son of man."*

Israel became a nation in a day when the Jews from around the world came together after two thousand years of wondering around. They returned to their homeland on May 14, 1948 fulfilling the ancient prophecy of Isaiah 66:78. I believe that's when the countdown to the Messiah's return began.

Within hours of the United Nations mandate expiring and ending British control of the land, the United States issued a statement recognising Israel's sovereignty. In essence, during a 24-hour span of time just as Isaiah foretold would happen, foreign control of the land of Israel formally ceased and Israel declared its independence. Her independence was also acknowledged by other nations. The rebirth of Israel literally occurred in a single day.

Just as the Bible predicted the birth of a nation in one day, there is a great harvest taking place today—and also a great falling away. God means what He said and He said what He means! We must therefore be aware of Satan's attempts to deceive—it is evident in the current division in the Church between simple grace and the greasy grace. The latter says I can sin anyway I want and never repent, while simple grace says I am accountable for my actions and must be humble to ask for and receive forgiveness.

Or, consider the attempts to rewrite Scripture—even by supposed men of God. When they do not like a particular verse, they will come up with all sorts of reasons to debate how this one verse or passage was implanted. Some have even gone as far as rewriting an entire book to meet their perceptions. Revelation 22:1819 talks about this very thing: *"For I testify unto every man that heareth the words of the prophecy of this book, If any man shall add unto these things, God shall add unto him the plagues that are written in this book: And if any man shall take away from the words of the book of this prophecy, God shall take away his part out of the book of life, and out of the holy city, and from the things which are written in this book."*

We often find proof of the Gospel from the earliest manuscripts that the same meanings and words remain faithful throughout history as promised in Matthew 5:18, *"For verily I say unto you, Till heaven and earth pass, one jot or one tittle shall in no wise pass from the law, till all be fulfilled."*

The Word Shall Prevail

Isaiah 40:8 *"The grass withereth, the flower fadeth: but the word of our God shall stand for ever."*

Isaiah 45:23 *"I have sworn by myself, the word is gone out of my mouth in righteousness, and shall not return, That unto me every knee shall bow, every tongue shall swear."*

Isaiah 55:11 *"So shall my word be that goeth forth out of my mouth: it shall not return unto me void, but it shall accomplish that which I please, and it shall prosper in the thing whereto I sent it."*

When I first started teaching and preaching about how unclean spirits like bitterness and unforgiveness were behind many sicknesses and diseases, I was amazed at how many people in the Church opposed it—even though this concept is taught in the Scriptures and confirmed by the latest medical research. For example, my dear friend Linda Lange and I wrote a book called What Was I Thinking? Even though it was endorsed by several physicians and many who read the book were healed, others still did not believe how one's thoughts influence one's body.

There was a German philosopher named Arthur Schopenhauer born in the late 1700s who said, "All truth passes through three stages. First, it is ridiculed. Secondly, it is violently opposed. Thirdly, it is accepted as being self-evident." So it is at times in the Church. Those of us within the prophecy movement have been accused of preaching and teaching science fiction and conspiracy theories. This saddens me as a pastor! I base everything I preach and teach on with the Bible. When should I or other Church leaders warn you of what's coming: before or after something happens? When did Noah warn his culture: before or after the flood?

You must ask yourself if you are running from this information because you are afraid. Let's not entertain the spirit of fear. It's the opposite of faith, and without faith, it is impossible to please the Lord, Romans 14:23. The fearful will find their end in the second death:

Revelation 21:8 *"But the fearful, and unbelieving, and the abominable, and murderers, and whoremongers, and sorcerers, and idolaters, and all liars, shall have their part in the lake which burneth with fire and brimstone: which is the second death."*

If "fearful" is listed with murderers, etc., then living in fear is pretty serious business. We are going to need to continue staying in faith and trust the Lord Jesus/Yeshua for all things as overcomers, even if it seems we have involuntarily been drafted into an episode of the Twilight Zone!

Now the Lord gave us insight as to when He would return for us.

Matthew 24:37-39 *"But as the days of Noah were, so shall also the coming of the Son of man be. [38]For as in the days that were before the flood they were eating and drinking, marrying and giving in marriage, until the day that Noah entered into the ark, [39]And knew not until the flood came, and took them all away; so shall also the coming of the Son of man be."*

What sorts of things were happening in the days of Noah? The Book of Genesis tells us that mankind was terribly wicked and that every imagination of the people's hearts also were evil. It must have been a very violent time on the earth—perhaps there were terrorist organisations as well. Even so, people were marrying and given in marriage. Some theologians have dug deep into the original language and discovered something interesting. They found that perversities and alternative lifestyles, which the Lord calls abominations, also abounded.

I believe the Word indicates there were also many evil spirits operating. We are told that angels came to earth and had sexual relations with women, creating a race of giants, or Nephilim. These were half animal and half human hybrids. Who knows if other assorted creatures were produced on this planet at that time? The Scriptures mention the Unicorn in Isaiah 34:7, *"And the unicorns shall come down with them, and the bullocks with the bulls; and their land shall be soaked with blood, and their dust made fat with fatness."*

The Religious Leaders said:

2) UFOs and related topics are very interesting, but as with MANY areas for discussion, do not directly build faith; they may actually increase fear.

First, let me just say that avoiding topics related to these things won't make them go away! Ready or not, after two thousand years of warning, this world is still not prepared for what is coming. But you are not "of this world." Believers can be ready without fear because we trust Jesus. Those who are not believers can choose to investigate the claims of the Bible and consider whether they might need a Saviour!

2 Thessalonians 2:8-12 *"And then shall that Wicked be revealed, whom the Lord shall consume with the spirit of his mouth, and shall destroy with the brightness of his coming: ⁹Even him, whose coming is after the working of Satan with all power and signs and lying wonders, ¹⁰And with all deceivableness of unrighteousness in them that perish; because they received not the love of the truth, that they might be saved. ¹¹And for this cause God shall send them strong delusion, that they should believe a lie: ¹²That they all might be damned who believed not the truth, but had pleasure in unrighteousness."*

After seeing scores of evidence to support such a position scripturally, I believe an extraterrestrial UFO deception may prove to be that strong delusion. Jesus does not want any of His followers to perish from lack of knowledge. Hosea 4:6, *"My people are destroyed for lack of knowledge: because thou hast rejected knowledge, I will also reject thee, that thou shalt be no priest to me: seeing thou hast forgotten the law of thy God, I will also forget thy children."*

So I would ask my pastor friend if he'd say that history, science, genetics, wars and rumours of wars, earthquakes, famine, the Middle East, Islam, trans humanism, homosexuality, trans genderism and related topics do not directly build faith, but may actually increase fear? They may and often do. But instead of running from these things, let's bring the promises of God into our understanding and then our faith will be built. Otherwise, we are in danger of becoming like the Church in Germany before WWII, ignoring Hitler and the Nazi's plans to destroy the Jews and Christians. Did the Church do then as these leaders are suggesting now? Did they simply ignore the Holy Word of God and only give a feel good, motivational message or conduct a religious ceremony? The Nazis attempted to unify Germany's Protestant churches under the Deutsche Christen movement, which rejected the Hebrew origins of the gospel. History shows us it was only after Hitler's death and after his evil empire had begun to crumble that the Roman Catholic Church finally disowned him.

The Nazi's SS modeled themselves after the Jesuit order. The Jesuits have their own ideas which are not biblically based and they now have a controlling interest in the Vatican and input at the highest levels worldwide.

Evidence has surfaced over the years that suggest Hitler and Eva Braun faked their suicides and actually escaped to Argentina. Hitler's remains were supposedly sent to Russia and forgotten about until in 2009, when Nicholas Bellatoni, an archeologist from Connecticut, was allowed to perform DNA testing on one of the skull fragments. The DNA did not match any recorded samples thought to be Hitler's, nor did they match Eva Braun's. That discovery set off a fire storm of questions that have never been answered, mainly, what did the Soviets actually discover in Hitler's Berlin bunker, could there have been a colossal cover-up, and why?

Avoiding reality doesn't work. Instead, we are supposed to learn a lesson from past mistakes.

The Religious Leaders said:

3) In this world, if you or I were publicly associated with the topic it would hurt, not help, our ministry of gospel proclamation because we would be perceived as "fringe religious."

Spirit-filled, born-again believers serve a God who is super-natural or "fringe." The Lord Jesus/Yeshua and His true disciples have always been and shall remain on the fringe if we truly pick up our crosses and follow Him. Matthew 16:2, *"Then said Jesus unto his disciples, If any man will come after me, let him deny himself, and take up his cross, and follow me."*

By His completed work it is possible for us to be made sin-less. There's no forgiveness, healing, restoration, deliverance, prosperity, or salvation without the cross and the supernatu-ral power of Jesus' resurrection. There are those who wonder how little of His precious blood they can get by with in their life. Yet, the blood represents the forgiveness of sins so person-ally, I want to continue standing under the cross of Christ my Messiah forever! Only by His blood and the word of our testi-mony are we able to become new creations in Christ Jesus (2 Corinthians 5:17, Rev. 10:11).

Besides, whose reputation are we supposed to be concerned about: the Lord's, or our own? Was Jesus ever concerned about what other may have thought about Him?

Philippians 2:7 *"But made himself of no reputation, and took upon him the form of a servant, and was made in the likeness of men:"*

Consider the original disciples and how they responded to attacks on their reputations:

Acts 5:27-29 *"And when they had brought them, they set them before the council: and the high priest asked them, [28]Say-ing, Did not we straitly command you that ye should not teach in this name? and, behold, ye have filled Jerusalem with your doctrine, and intend to bring this man's blood upon us. [29]Then Peter and the other apostles answered and said, We ought to obey God rather than men."*

Joshua and Caleb were the only two of twelve spies sent into the land who came back with a positive report. When they saw the giants they believed God Almighty would give them the supernatural power and ability to succeed. As a result of their faith, Joshua and Caleb were the only men from their entire generation actually permitted to go into the Promised Land. It appears the rest of the Israelites forgot about all the supernatural provision and protection they enjoyed at that time: their shoes and clothing never wore out and the Lord provided supernatural food (manna), and made water gush forth from a rock.

Deuteronomy 8:4 *"Thy raiment waxed not old upon thee, neither did thy foot swell, these forty years."*

Again, it was the "fringe" Israelis who went into the Promised Land.

If we are more concerned about what people think of us, then perhaps we have given into the spirit of fear, which is not from God. "For God hath not given us the spirit of fear; but of power, and of love, and of a sound mind" (2 Timothy 1:7).

The fear of being considered kooky, wacko, or fringe represents ungodly thinking coming from an anti God spirit. When it merges with your thought life, it builds up strongholds in your thinking that hinder you. Ephesians 6:12 tells us, "For we wrestle not against flesh and blood, but against principalities, against powers, against the rulers of the darkness of this world, against spiritual wickedness in high places."

These dark, fearful, and toxic thoughts always project into the future with questions like "What if _____?" (You can fill in the blank.) The result is a thought life filled with anxiety, stress, and a complete lack of peace. What starts in your mind eventually manifests in your body with things such as stomach issues, heart disease, and neurological disorders. I have taken time towards the end of this book to explain more about how we can take control of fearful thoughts and cast them down in order to live in peace. I think you will find that section liberating!

The Religious Leaders said:

4) The Truth that sets us free is Jesus, not every bit of truth on any issue. Even knowing "truth" may take our focus off the Lord.

I must admit I am a perplexed that anyone would think that knowing the truth could ever take your focus off the Lord. He is the way, the truth and the life (John 14:6).

Let us always go by the Word of God instead of the words of men. For the Lord Jesus said in John 8:31-32, "*... If ye continue in my word, then are ye my disciples indeed; And ye shall know the truth, and the truth shall make you free.*"

It appears to me this suggestion that we don't need to know all the truth is shaded in various degrees of darkness and fear. John 3:19 says, "*And this is the condemnation, that light is come into the world, and men loved darkness rather than light, because their deeds were evil.*"

From my understanding of the Holy Scriptures, Papa God is saying that when your heart is darkened you will do what you consider to be good, even though it is evil according to the Lord. However, if you have a heart to be righteous because you want to please the Lord, you will act according to your faith. Now you will do good with the right motives and have His supernatural protection.

For we read in places like Hebrews 11:6, "*But without faith it is impossible to please him: for he that cometh to God must believe that he is, and that he is a rewarder of them that diligently seek him.*"

May the Lord use and bless you always as you diligently seek Him, His kingdom, and His righteousness!

The Religious Leaders said:

5) This is not from God.

I could not agree with them more on this! It is precisely my point that UFOs, trans humanism, demonic activity, and so on are clearly not from God. So what would the Lord have us do about it? Shall the Church remain clueless as to what is taking place because we were more concerned about being considered "fringe"?

I believe we are already seeing the impact the alien/UFO deception is having on the world. The growing number of Christians I have met over the years who have actually taken the time to study the Scriptures to show themselves approved and have researched the extraterrestrial phenomena, often arrive at a similar conclusion. Like Noah who warned people before the flood, I want to help as many people as possible make their peace with the Lord Jesus before it's too late. When Jesus began healing the sick, it brought Him much trouble from the religious leaders of His time. But did he stop? No. He continued out of pure love for them. True believers need the same love and concern that Jesus showed, doing what God asks of us. Jesus never said or did anything without hearing it from his Father first. Because I am privileged to have this same love for the brethren, I am compelled to share all that the Lord has laid upon my heart concerning these deceptions.

Come, let us reason together... (Isaiah 1:18).

I believe we can expect to experience a steady, ongoing increase in both the severity and scope of these lying signs and wonders. At some appointed time in the future, full disclosure shall most likely happen. When it does, and if the Church is still here, we may find that the extraterrestrial/UFO phenomena is much more dangerous for the Church than Islam and Muslim Jihadists ever thought about being.

The Religious Leaders said:

> 6) Some even ventured, that if offered at another location, they might even attend, and that it might be helpful for leaders to attend, but not for all the folks and definitely not at church.

This really sounds to me that these trusted advisors are entertaining the spirit of fear. You may recall the account of Nicodemus who was so fearful that he secretly went to see Jesus at night so no one would see him (John 3:13). Isn't it interesting that these religious leaders feel only they should be made aware of these lying signs and wonders manifesting all round the world? This sounds like the Dark Ages, where Church leaders were solely privy to the scriptures and taught congregations their interpretation. Perhaps some religions are still trying to do that today! But the Lord sees through everything, even to the thoughts and intents of the heart (1 Samuel 16:7).

Now, I certainly understand that leaders in the church are to protect the Lord's flock; however, we read in 1 Peter 2:9, *"But ye are a chosen generation, a royal priesthood, an holy nation, a peculiar people; that ye should shew forth the praises of him who hath called you out of darkness into his marvellous light."* This was spoken about the entire body of Christ. We are taught to study, search out a matter, and memorise and meditate on the Word. I know many churches don't encourage people to bring their Bibles to church and instead use a Power Point to display the verses. Many use unauthorized versions. How will the flock know when they are being force fed—or when great sections of important doctrine are being left out?

As the Word says, the body should be edified by those the Lord supplies.

Ephesians 4:11-12 *"And he gave some, apostles; and some, prophets; and some, evangelists; and some, pastors and teachers; 12 For the perfecting of the saints, for the work of the ministry, for the edifying of the body of Christ:"*

My prayer is that the Lord will open hearts, eyes and ears to the truth before it's too late.

Acts 26:18 *"To open their eyes, and to turn them from darkness to light, and from the power of Satan unto God, that they may receive forgiveness of sins, and inheritance among them which are sanctified by faith that is in me."*

I believe fear is the biggest reason the Church today has not been edified and equipped to understand the end-times. As you saw from the letter, these religious mentioned fear several times: they are afraid for their reputations, they are afraid of certain kinds of truth, and they are afraid for God's people. They are so afraid they seek to limit even those things that would help us prepare for what's coming. Yet, lack of information is what God calls ignorance, and says His people perish from it.

Hosea 4:6 *"My people are destroyed for lack of knowledge: because thou hast rejected knowledge, I will also reject thee, that thou shalt be no priest to me: seeing thou hast forgotten the law of thy God, I will also forget thy children."*

Now, that's not to say that we are to allow ourselves to be spoon-fed. In fact, we should carefully sift through what's out there so we can separate out the truth, asking the Lord for discernment to help us tell the difference.

There appears to be a great deal of misinformation and propaganda circulating today devoted to purposefully confuse us about UFOs, Nephilim, and alien abductions. This is the atmosphere in which the spirit of fear loves to operate. The study of ufology—which is the investigation of evidence related to UFOs—includes reports of extraterrestrials, flying saucers, cattle mutilations, alien abductions, and implants. These things leave many people scratching their heads trying to find the truth.

There is also this erroneous concept that truth can be divided: one side of truth is accessed by reason and evidence, whilst the other side is based on blind faith. This idea has now infiltrated our society to the point people that say such absurd things as, "That may be the truth for you, but it is not the truth for me." Faith is neither blind nor is it wishful thinking; rather, faith is based on evidence we can trust. And if it is not the truth, could we just call it a lie? The Lord Jesus said to Pilate in John 18:37, *"Every one that is of the truth heareth my voice."*

Pilate responded, "What is truth?" Obviously Pilate was on the wrong side in this philosophical debate.

Jesus Christ of Nazareth was either resurrected and is the only begotten Son of God or He is not! The apostle Paul presented us with profound truth in 1 Corinthians 15:14, *"And if Christ be not risen, then is our preaching vain, and your faith is also vain."*

We are seeing a great divide happening today between the apostate superficial churches and the supernatural churches. The time has come for separating the goats from the sheep. Here is the gospel truth: Jesus Christ of Nazareth, being born a man, came to earth and bore our sins, died on the cross and rose again, and when He returns He is going to set up a new Heaven and new Earth. (Acts 1:11, Rev. 21:14)

How close are we to the edge of time? How prepared are you for world changes and the coming great deception? We are instructed about the dangers of ignorance in places like

Proverbs 22:3, *"A prudent man foreseeth the evil, and hideth himself: but the simple pass on, and are punished."* Remember, Noah was one of the first "preppers." And the best way to be a prepper is to be right with the Lord. Genesis 7:1 says, *"And the LORD said unto Noah, Come thou and all thy house into the ark; for thee have I seen righteous before me in this generation."*

Furthermore, without Jesus, it is pointless to do much of anything!

John 15:5, *"I am the vine, ye are the branches: He that abideth in me, and I in him, the same bringeth forth much fruit: for without me ye can do nothing."*

We are told that the world shall be about their respective business until suddenly the Lord of Glory shall appear. One must seriously ask, "Am I prepared to meet Jesus Christ of Nazareth?"

All the unbelievers will suddenly realise the foolishness of what they have done and find themselves in everlasting mourning, whilst repenting sinners shall look to the Lord Jesus and be eternally overjoyed. Those showing no regret or sorrow for their sins and misbehaviours shall also see Him. Even though they laugh disrespectfully now, they shall find themselves in that day weeping in utter despair. Although the elect of God are scattered throughout the earth, when the Lord sends His angels at the day of the great gathering, not one of those saved shall be left behind!

Matthew 24:30 *"And then shall appear the sign of the Son of man in heaven: and then shall all the tribes of the earth mourn, and they shall see the Son of man coming in the clouds of heaven with power and great glory."*

At some point in the near future, it will be proven to all the unsaved scoffers and skeptics alike that Jesus Christ of Nazareth/Messiah Yeshua is real. The appearance of Antichrist and the completion of all events heralding the return of Christ may very well occur in this present generation. He is who He said He is. What shall you therefore say to skeptics? Please tell them that born-again, Spirit-filled believers only have to be right once!

Mark 13:27 *"And then shall he send his angels, and shall gather together his elect from the four winds, from the uttermost part of the earth to the uttermost part of heaven."*

Perhaps you are reading this book because you have decided that it is time to begin looking at these subjects. Perhaps you are one who would like to be presented with the available evidence so that you can draw your own conclusions. I hope this book will give you the material you need to assess the situation, provide names of additional resources so you can do greater research, if desired, and encourage you with God's direction for making the most of the time, because the days are short.

Chapter Three

UFOS AND ALIENS

Let us consider the many distractions and assorted red herrings on the scene sent to confuse us. We were warned in places like Galatians 1:8, *"But though we, or an angel from heaven, preach any other gospel unto you than that which we have preached unto you, let him be accursed."*

What is the truth then about these numerous reports of space aliens that have manifested? Are they actually superiour intelligent beings who designed and created mankind on planet Earth? I will give you my opinion and the opinion of others. Again, I want to stress that this is just the merest glimpse into these topics. I encourage you to research these things for yourself and come to your own conclusions.

Outspoken experts of atheism as Sir. Richard Dawkins and New Age philosophers seem to think aliens from another dimension have invaded our planet. Others, such as this author, believe these beings are actually demonic entities masquerading as extraterrestrials. I have personally heard reports by adults and children who claim to have been abducted by aliens against their will. In many instances, these people say they were sexually violated and traumatised, and their eggs or sperm taken from them during the course of these abductions. Some of the women say they were impregnated by ETs and later discovered that they miscarried (fetuses seem to have mysteriously disappeared from their wombs).

There are reports by people claiming to have been abducted numerous times since childhood. L. A. Marzulli, with his quick wit and humour, calls them "frequent flyers." Marzulli and his colleagues Richard Shaw, Tom Horn, Cris Putnam, Russ Dizdar, Russ Berault, Gary Stearman, and others have helped me pursue writing this book. Marzulli has the heart for the things of God and it is his (and my) desire to help prepare anyone who is willing to listen for what is surely coming in the near future. We have worked together in conferences and ministered to numbers of people who have been victimised by the enemy of our souls, seeing many restored as only the Lord Jesus can do.

We believe there is now a deceptive worldwide agenda misleading people and ushering in a totalitarian New World Order. Corrupted world leaders and shadow governments, perhaps with extraterrestrials (what I believe are demons). I believe they are working today in underground bases and military installations to overturn order and bring in utter chaos.

Revelation 1:3 *"Blessed is he that readeth, and they that hear the words of this prophecy, and keep those things which are written therein: for the time is at hand."*

In part, my quest began with this question, What did Jesus mean when he said, *"But as the days of Noah were, so shall also the coming of the Son of man be"?* (Matt. 24:37) They were eating and drinking, marrying and giving in marriage and were unaware of what was coming.

The world of that day was also overrun with great evil. The flood appears to have happened rather suddenly, yet the Lord issued plenty of warnings. Few got on the ark then, and few will be ultimately saved when the end comes, because mankind doesn't want to follow the narrow way. Matthew 7:14 says, *"Because strait is the gate, and narrow is the way, which leadeth unto life, and few there be that find it."*

We read in Genesis 6 that Noah was a blameless man, which must mean he certainly lived in a way that was honouring the Lord. Furthermore, Noah was a preacher of righteousness:

2 Peter 2:5 *"And spared not the old world, but saved Noah the eighth person, a preacher of righteousness, bringing in the flood upon the world of the ungodly;"*

We only have a small glimpse of Noah's activities in the days leading up to the flood, but we can make a reasonable assumption he preached about it to his neighbours and anyone who would listen. It took Noah and his sons 100 years to complete and ready the ark. I suppose he must have really seemed an odd chap in his day, building such an extreme structure of a ship. So when the Lord calls us a "peculiar people," we ought to feel better about it! (1 Peter 2:9)

Matt. 24:38-39 *"For as in the days that were before the flood they were eating and drinking, marrying and giving in marriage, until the day that Noe entered into the ark, ³⁹And knew not until the flood came, and took them all away; so shall also the coming of the Son of man be."*

As you consider this parallel, you may be wondering if all sins are equal before the Lord. And, Just how narrow is the narrow gate? Contrary to what we are being told by some pastors and Christian leaders today, there is no other way to enter into heaven except by salvation through Jesus Christ of Nazareth (John 14:6). Few are willing to meet the requirements today. We read in James 5:19-20, *"Brethren, if any of you do err from the truth, and one convert him; Let him know, that he which converteth the sinner from the error of his way shall save a soul from death, and shall hide a multitude of sins."*

Now before we get too deeply into this, please keep in mind that there are those in certain dominations who profess to be born again Christians and yet they basically deny that Jesus is the same, yesterday, today and forever (see Hebrews 13:8). They want to pick and choose which Scriptures are important, and may eliminate whole parts of the Bible. Yet, 2 Timothy 3:16 tells us that, *"All scripture is given by inspiration of God, and is profitable for doctrine, for reproof, for correction, for instruction in righteousness."*

Many Christians erroneously take the position that some of the gifts of the Holy Spirit are no longer functional, such as healing and miracles or speaking in unknown languages. They somehow think these things passed away 2,000 years ago when the last of the original apostles died. When did God stop producing apostles? Did they die out with the prophets? Who took them out of Ephesians 4:11? *"And he gave some, apostles; and some, prophets; and some, evangelists; and some, pastors and teachers; For the perfecting of the saints, for the work of the ministry, for the edifying of the body of Christ."* Since they are all in the same sentence, surely the Lord produces all of them in every succeeding generation.

Those who believe the gifts and the appointing of prophets passed away may also encounter some difficulty understanding verses regarding the days of Noah. For the Lord clearly says in places like Mark 16 that these signs shall follow those who believe: casting out demons, laying hands on the sick so they recover, and raising the dead. If you don't believe these things are possible, then nothing much in that dimension shall happen for you. In fact, Jesus said we must believe in order to receive. Matthew 21:22 *"And all things, whatsoever ye shall ask in prayer, believing, ye shall receive."*

Those who want to tell us that the gifts of prophecy, tongues, healing, and miracles have passed away should be asked if knowledge has passed away as well? If knowledge has not passed away, then neither did the gift of the Holy Spirit—including tongues—vanish away. Notice that these things are all listed in one sentence. 1 Corinthians 13:8 *"Charity never faileth: but whether there be prophecies, they shall fail; whether there be tongues, they shall cease; whether there be knowledge, it shall vanish away."*

Strange Creatures in Noah's Day

The days of Noah included the existence of the race of giants. This was a genetic corruption to the seed of mankind that occurred when fallen angels (also called watchers) had relationship with human women.

Genesis 6:24 *"That the sons of God saw the daughters of men that they were fair; and they took them wives of all which they chose. And the LORD said, My spirit shall not always strive with man, for that he also is flesh: yet his days shall be an hundred and twenty years. There were giants in the earth in those days; and also after that, when the sons of God came in unto the daughters of men, and they bare children to them, the same became mighty men which were of old, men of renown."*

Some might speculate that these were extraterrestrials who invaded the earth before the flood of Noah and managed to contaminate all human DNA except Noah and his family. Others believe this to be the work of the fallen angels or demons—corrupting what the Lord made by changing the pure human line from Adam to create genetic hybrids. We might ask if these demonic beings masquerading as aliens understood genetic splicing—what is now called trans humanism.

Genesis 6:56 *"And GOD saw that the wickedness of man was great in the earth, and that every imagination of the thoughts of his heart was only evil continually. 6And it repented the LORD that he had made man on the earth, and it grieved him at his heart."*

The Holy Scriptures say this genetic corruption also happened again AFTER the flood (Gen. 6:4). I believe much of Greek Mythology is based upon these types of beings. Interestingly, the Lord instructs His people to destroy the Nephilim in the land they would go to possess. If we don't understand that these evil beings were not supposed to have been created, we could misunderstand the love of God. The biggest issue some unsaved people have is God's command to kill women, children and animals in those lands. It might change their opinion if these were demonically created beings not meant to be here!

I believe we are already seeing the impact the alien/UFO deception is having on the world today. Ever since the former Canadian Minister of Defense, the honourable Paul Hellyer (who certainly had access to top secret information most people be denied), stated on record at the 2013 Congressional Disclosures Meetings, "UFOs are as real as airplanes flying overhead."

As the birth pangs get closer and more severe, I think we will experience a steady increase in these lying signs and wonders. At some appointed time in the future, full disclosure shall most likely happen. When it does, and if the Church is still here, it will severely alter most of our perceptions of reality. For that reason, I believe the extraterrestrial/UFO phenomena is much more dangerous than run-of-the-mill false religions such as ISIS. The extraterrestrial/UFO phenomena has a veneer of scientific credibility, since celebrated scientists like physicist Stephen Hawking have given it credence.

Consider also the well-known atheistic evolutionist Richard Dawkins. In 2008, while being interviewed for the documentary film Expelled: No Intelligence Allowed, Dawkins admitted that he did not understand where the first self replicating molecule came from, however he thinks superior intelligent beings from some other civilization, evolved in a Darwinian way, came here and started life as we know it.

Another scientist, Sir Francis Crick—codiscoverer of the DNA molecule—theorized that life originated in outer space. He posited that microorganisms, or some chemical precursors of life, were able to initiate life upon reaching a suitable environment like Earth. Many scientists have been programmed to believe this is a logical explanation for the complex code found on human DNA.

Did you know that the Vatican is heading up a project called "L.U.C.I.F.E.R."? This is a Large Binocular Telescope Nearinfrared Utility with Camera and Integral Field Unit for Extragalactic Research. I should think these astronomers must be observing some rather spectacular scenes from the Milky Way to extremely distant galaxies. LUCIFER is situated on Mt. Graham in Arizona and is presumed to be a gateway, or portal, that things from other dimensions use to come and go—something like what the angels were doing in the account of Jacob's ladder.

Vatican scientist Guy Consolmagno suggested in 2010 that aliens might have souls and therefore could be baptized if they asked for it. Father Giuseppe Tanzella Nitti is the Vactican's Eminent Theologian and Full Professor of Fundamental Theology at the Pontificia Università della Santa Croce in Rome. He said, "Christians will not immediately need to renounce their faith in God simply on the basis of the reception of [this] new unexpected information of a religious character from extraterrestrial civilizations. However, once the "religious content" originating from outside the Earth "has been verified" they will have to conduct "a rereading [of the Gospel] inclusive of the new data."

Now why is the Vatican so concerned with astrobiology? Astrobiology is concerned with the effects of outer space on living organisms and searching for extraterrestrial life. It encompasses areas of biology, astronomy, and geology. One definition I found interesting was this: (1) understanding the conditions under which life can arise, (2) looking for habitable worlds, and (3) searching for evidence of life.

I am reminded here of Galatians 1:8, *"But though we, or an angel from heaven, preach any other gospel unto you than that which we have preached unto you, let him be accursed."*

Do we think Satan has just been trying to get people to lie and cheat and steal? Satan has had thousands of years to plan ahead and formulate what is happening today.

There is a very dangerous doctrine being presented today that says Jesus of Nazareth was actually some sort of highly evolved and advanced extraterrestrial! It was His technological prowess that gave Him the ability to heal the sick, perform miracles, and raise the dead. We are already seeing the merging of occultism with traditional Christian beliefs. It seems at every conference I have done we have met individuals needing prayer and ministry who have been victimised by some encounter with an entity that they claimed be from another planet. Others want to share their experience about having seen something in the sky that they have no explanation for. Almost without exception, they have admitted to never being able to feel safe enough before to tell anyone, not even their pastors or church leaders, for fear of being ridiculed.

However, belief in the coming extraterrestrial saviour is so prevalent today that the majority of people in Western nations, including UK and USA, believe that over the Holy Word of God. If the church does not understand the great deception, it will be seen as irrelevant. Mark my words, these lying signs and wonders are going to continue to escalate in the future. There is clearly an agenda in place to break down our resistance that society will accept this conditioning of our culture. After all, the Lord Jesus forewarned us of this time when people would no longer endure sound doctrine.

Matthew 24:24-25 *"For there shall arise false Christs, and false prophets, and shall shew great signs and wonders; insomuch that, if it were possible, they shall deceive the very elect. Behold, I have told you before."*

How dangerous will it be if we choose to ignore such information or neglect to study and show ourselves approved of the Lord! We are seeing a great divide today between the apostate, superficial churches and the supernatural churches. Here is the gospel truth: Jesus Christ of Nazareth being born a man came to earth and bore our sins, died on the cross and rose again. When He returns He will set up a new heaven and new earth.

Acts 1:11 *"Which also said, Ye men of Galilee, why stand ye gazing up into heaven? this same Jesus, which is taken up from you into heaven, shall so come in like manner as ye have seen him go into heaven."*

Revelation 21:1-4 *"And I saw a new heaven and a new earth: for the first heaven and the first earth were passed away; and there was no more sea. ²And I John saw the holy city, new Jerusalem, coming down from God out of heaven, prepared as a bride adorned for her husband. ³And I heard a great voice out of heaven saying, Behold, the tabernacle of God is with men, and he will dwell with them, and they shall be his people, and God himself shall be with them, and be their God.⁴And God shall wipe away all tears from their eyes; and there shall be no more death, neither sorrow, nor crying, neither shall there be any more pain: for the former things are passed away."*

How close are we to the edge of time? How prepared are you for world changes and the coming great deception? *"A prudent man foreseeth the evil, and hideth himself: but the simple pass on, and are punished"* (Proverbs 22:3). Remember, Noah was one of the first "preppers." So the best way to be a prepper is to be in Christ. John 15:5 *"I am the vine, ye are the branches: He that abideth in me, and I in him, the same bringeth forth much fruit: for without me ye can do nothing."*

Keep looking up, my friend, and understand the times and the prophecies which are unfolding as the sheep are separated from the goats. How soon will the day come in which we are asked to renounce our faith?

Nephilim's Presence after the Flood

The Lord Jesus foretells that His second coming shall be as it was in Noah's day. Genesis 6:4 *"There were giants in the earth in those days; and also after that, when the sons of God came in unto the daughters of men, and they bare children to them, the same became mighty men which were of old, men of renown."*

This indicates that the Nephilim—half-demons, half-human hybrids born out of a union between fallen angels and women of Earth—would also return again after the flood of Noah. The word Nephilim goes much deeper and darker than just mere gigantism with six fingers on each hand, six toes on each foot, and double rows of teeth. Nephilim became synonyms with giants, however, it is no way limited to simply meaning only giants. It is a basic term that connotes the biological offspring of flesh and blood beings with fallen angel beings.

As we study the Lord's plan for mankind, we are made aware of the agenda of the evil one throughout the Holy Bible. We are watching the ancient prophecies unfold as never before and we are also seeing a sinister plot in place to convince as many people as possible that Jesus Christ of Nazareth was not who He has absolutely proven to be. There is an agenda to suggest that Jesus was just an ordinary man who was aided by extraterrestrials or created by them and given supernatural powers and attempt to explain how Jesus performed miracles. Perhaps the enemy will try to convince the world that Jesus was actually an extraterrestrial, performing lying signs and wonders.

However, there is no evidence of any extraterrestrials ever healing the blind, deaf and lame, raising the dead and performing the sort of miracles that Jesus Christ of Nazareth did and continues to do through His disciples throughout the ages in every generation. Besides, where in the Bible did the Lord ever stop performing miracles if He is always the same?

Hebrews 13:8 *"Jesus Christ the same yesterday, and to day, and for ever."*

Malachi 3:6 *"For I am the LORD, I change not; therefore ye sons of Jacob are not consumed."*

There are cases where someone stopped an alien abduction by commanding it to cease in the almighty name of Jesus. So aliens respond just as demons do (hint, hint), which begs the question: Are these really from another planet or are they demons that have to submit to the name of Jesus? Selah

Luke 10:19 *"Behold, I give unto you power to tread on serpents and scorpions, and over all the power of the enemy: and nothing shall by any means hurt you."*

I find it fascinating to observe how all these things Bible prophecies predicted to happen before Jesus returns are happening right now. Do not fear, keep in mind that whatever the devil attempts, the Lord our God will always outmaneuver. No matter who the enemy controls behind the scenes or what they do, it will only fulfill Bible prophecy and they will lose in the end.

"For we shall all stand before the judgment seat of Christ" (2 Corinthians 5:10).

"And as it is appointed unto men once to die, but after this the judgment" (Hebrews 9:27).

All the world shall be about their respective businesses and suddenly the Lord of Glory shall appear. In that moment every heart on earth shall turn inward and announce, "It is the Lord!" One must seriously ask, "Am I prepared to meet Jesus Christ of Nazareth?"

All the sinners of the world will suddenly realise the foolishness of what they have done and find themselves in everlasting mourning; whilst repenting sinners shall look to the Lord Jesus and be overwhelmed in His Holiness and they shall be eternally overjoyed. Impenitent sinners showing no regret or sorrow for their sins and misbehaviours shall also see Christ whom they have pierced, and even though they laugh disrespectfully now, they shall find themselves weeping in endless horror.

Although the elect of God are scattered throughout the earth, when the Lord sends His angels at the day of the great gathering, not one of those saved shall be left behind!

Romans 8:16-18 *"The Spirit itself beareth witness with our spirit, that we are the children of God: 17And if children, then heirs; heirs of God, and joint heirs with Christ; if so be that we suffer with him, that we may be also glorified together. 18For I reckon that the sufferings of this present time are not worthy to be compared with the glory which shall be revealed in us."*

Mark 13:27 *"And then shall he send his angels, and shall gather together his elect from the four winds, from the uttermost part of the earth to the uttermost part of heaven."*

Matthew 24:30 *"And then shall appear the sign of the Son of man in heaven: and then shall all the tribes of the earth mourn, and they shall see the Son of man coming in the clouds of heaven with power and great glory."*

Romans 8:17 *"And if children, then heirs; heirs of God, and joint heirs with Christ; if so be that we suffer with him, that we may be also glorified together."*

I pray that you are inspired to make your paths straight before the Lord. And if you feel backslidden in any area of your life as a professing Christian, I pray you will come before the Lord Jesus/Yeshua in true tears of repentance and receive His amazingly awesome mercy, grace, love, and forgiveness.

"But be ye doers of the word, and not hearers only, deceiving your own selves" (James 1:22).

"If we confess our sins, he is faithful and just to forgive us our sins, and to cleanse us from all unrighteousness. If we say that we have not sinned, we make him a liar, and his word is not in us" (1 John 1:9 10).

Don't wait even one hour to turn your life over to Him.

The wise men of ancient days we call the Magi saw the signs that the Messiah would soon be born and went to find him. They were probably scholars from the order that originated with the prophet Daniel and remained in Babylon after the exile. The Magi would have understood the Old Testament prophecies and likely studied other related ancient manuscripts from around the world. Matthew 2:2 says, *"Where is he that is born King of the Jews? for we have seen his star in the east, and are come to worship him."*

In Numbers 24:17, *"Balaam referred to a star coming out of Jacob, "I shall see him, but not now: I shall behold him, but not nigh: there shall come a Star out of Jacob, and a Sceptre shall rise out of Israel, and shall smite the corners of Moab, and destroy all the children of Sheth."*

We have multiple explanations of what the Star actually was, but whatever it was, the Magi rode horses thousand of miles led by the star to find the Messiah. How far are we prepared to go to meet with the Lord today when He is only a prayer away?

Just to set the record straight, baby Jesus was probably close to being one or even two years old when the Magi finally found Him. By this time Joseph and Mary were married and living in a house in Bethlehem. Matthew 2:9 "When they had heard the king, they departed; and, lo, the star, which they saw in the east, went before them, till it came and stood over where the young child was." The Greek word for "young child" can actually mean anything from a newborn infant to a toddler.

Matthew 2:11 *"And when they were come into the house, they saw the young child with Mary his mother, and fell down, and worshipped him: and when they had opened their treasures, they presented unto him gifts; gold, and frankincense and myrrh."*

Note that they came to a house, not a stable. Joseph naturally would have moved his young family to a more protected place as soon as possible regardless of the rumours that may have followed them about his wife and child. In fact, they may have needed to stay in Bethlehem because we read in Luke 2:22, *"And when the days of her purification according to the law of Moses were accomplished, they brought him to Jerusalem, to present him to the Lord;"*

So Joseph and Mary almost surely stayed in Bethlehem until Mary could once again travel. They probably stayed there for at least the 40 days necessary to complete Mary's purification process. They could make the five mile trip from Bethlehem to Jerusalem for the sacrifice for Mary's purification. Then Joseph was instructed in a dream to take his family to Egypt to avoid the wrath of Herod who had all young male children killed. This is the devil using Herod to try and kill the promised Messiah before His time (Matthew 2:13).

It is also interesting to note the expensive gifts that the Magi gave—worthy acknowledgements for the future King of Kings and Lord of Lords. All these gifts had special meaning as the Lord's attributes were revealed to the Magi's through careful study of the Word of God. They presented baby Jesus with gold to acknowledge His royalty, incense to acknowledge His deity, and myrrh (a spice for someone who is about to die) to acknowledge that Jesus would die for the sins of the world. Perhaps the Lord had the Magi present these gifts to also help finance their escape to Egypt.

The Lord warned the Magi as well in Matthew 2:12, *"And being warned of God in a dream that they should not return to Herod, they departed into their own country another way."*

My point in sharing this is to help us realise just as the devil was not able to find baby Jesus, God will protect us from what is to come. He is all-knowing and almighty and the devil is not. 1 Corinthians 2:8 *"Which none of the princes of this world knew: for had they known it, they would not have crucified the Lord of glory."*

The Magi read and believed the Word of the Lord enough to seek after baby Jesus. They recognised the value of serving Christ and humbled themselves and worshipped Him. They also understood it was better to obey God than man, and so outmaneuvered Herod. They were indeed wise men who didn't fear man! They continued seeking the child no matter what. Are we willing to do the same today? Nothing much has changed; evil is still evil, and we have the same choices to make as they did 2000 years ago. Let us learn from this and apply it to our lives today.

The wise Biblical student sees the signs for the second coming of Jesus Christ of Nazareth. As Jesus Christ Himself instructed us in Luke 21:36, *"Watch ye therefore, and pray always, that ye may be accounted worthy to escape all these things that shall come to pass, and to stand before the Son of man."*

We read a few verses before this in Luke 21:31-32, *"So likewise ye, when ye see these things come to pass, know ye that the kingdom of God is nigh at hand. Verily I say unto you, This generation shall not pass away, till all be fulfilled."*

No one can tell us with certainly when the exact timing of Jesus' return shall be except our Heavenly Father. Matthew 24:36, *"But of that day and hour knoweth no man, no, not the angels of heaven, but my Father only."*

I am reminded of Luke 9:24, *"For whosoever will save his life shall lose it: but whosoever will lose his life for my sake, the same shall save it."* You are either moving away from the gospel truth of Jesus/Yeshua or you are drawing closer to Him. We need to see past the moment when we breathe our last breath into the place where we will spend the majority of our lives—eternity. Think about it. We live in a supernatural world and the fact that eternity is more than anyone can ever imagine. Maybe if we could compare the parts of an atom with the size of an ever expanding universe we may catch a glimpse of what the Lord has planned for those who love Him. No matter how you have failed in your life, the Lord tells us His love is everlasting. He paid an untold price to make a way for sinners to be saved.

Mark 2:17 *"When Jesus heard it, he saith unto them, They that are whole have no need of the physician, but they that are sick: I came not to call the righteous, but sinners to repentance."*

Signs of the Times

Which brings us back to what Jesus said in Matthew 24:6-14, *"And ye shall hear of wars and rumours of wars: see that ye be not troubled: for all these things must come to pass, but the end is not yet. ⁷For nation shall rise against nation, and kingdom against kingdom: and there shall be famines, and pestilences, and earthquakes, in divers places.⁸All these are the beginning of sorrows. ⁹Then shall they deliver you up to be afflicted, and shall kill you: and ye shall be hated of all nations for my name's sake. ¹⁰And then shall many be offended, and shall betray one another, and shall hate one another. ¹¹And many false prophets shall rise, and shall deceive many. ¹²And because iniquity shall abound, the love of many shall wax cold. 13But he that shall endure unto the end, the same shall be saved. 14And this gospel of the kingdom shall be preached in all the world for a witness unto all nations; and then shall the end come."*

As all these things are lining up, will the "MYSTERY, BABYLON THE GREAT, THE MOTHER OF HARLOTS AND ABOMINATIONS OF THE EARTH" from Rev. 17:5 soon be revealed? Will a powerful religious leader come forward to announce how we have all been misled? Will we be told that historically, from the beginning of time, extraterrestrials began all life on this planet and are now here to help save the world from its destructive ways?

This could be what causes all religions to be merged into one: the religion of the new globalisation. Then, demonic beings masquerading as extraterrestrials will offer stunning new technology—such as a microchip that, once inserted into your hand or forehead, will begin changing your DNA and keep you from contracting sickness and disease? Perhaps they will promise to extend the average life span to over 900 years, just like in the days of Noah. This may all sound like scifi, but there is a new compound chemical called Nicotinamide Adenine Dinucleotide (NAD) that can make old cells young again. A microchip could be passed off as the key to health and the fountain of youth.

How many people will readily accept such an offer? How many will be caught off guard because no one warned them ahead of time to prepare them for this deception? Personally, I do not want to stand before the Lord Jesus/Yeshua one day and try and explain why I did not fully share such information and help prepare those with willing hearts to draw closer to the Lord.

We read of a time that will surely come when people will want to die and not be able to, as told in Revelation 6:15-17:

"15And the kings of the earth, and the great men, and the rich men, and the chief captains, and the mighty men, and every bondman, and every free man, hid themselves in the dens and in the rocks of the mountains; 16And said to the mountains and rocks, Fall on us, and hide us from the face of him that sitteth on the throne, and from the wrath of the Lamb: 17For the great day of his wrath is come; and who shall be able to stand?"

This certainly appears to indicate a day is coming when people will say to the mountains and rocks, "fall on us," choosing death rather than life. Because who will be able to stand in the day of the wrath of the Lord Jesus?

The Lord Jesus will be triumphant, just as He conquered death on the cross before He was gloriously resurrected.

The resurrected Lord Jesus appeared to over 500 people and told them to wait in Jerusalem for the Holy Ghost to come on them, yet only 120 waited.

Paul writes in 1 Corinthians 15:68 *"After that, he was seen of above five hundred brethren at once; of whom the greater part remain unto this present, but some are fallen asleep. 7After that, he was seen of James; then of all the apostles. 8And last of all he was seen of me also, as of one born out of due time.*

What shall become of the Antichrist and his deranged side-kick, the false prophet, you dare ask? He shall be cast into the everlasting lake of fire after the Lord's Millennium reign.

Revelation 19:20 *"And the beast was taken, and with him the false prophet that wrought miracles before him, with which he deceived them that had received the mark of the beast, and them that worshipped his image. These both were cast alive into a lake of fire burning with brimstone."*

I have wonderful news to share because we also read about the 'catching up together with the Lord' commonly called the "Rapture" for true believers in 1 Thessalonians 4:16-18, *"For the Lord himself shall descend from heaven with a shout, with the voice of the archangel, and with the trump of God: and the dead in Christ shall rise first: ¹⁷Then we which are alive and remain shall be caught up together with them in the clouds, to meet the Lord in the air: and so shall we ever be with the Lord. ¹⁸Wherefore comfort one another with these words."*

I pray what I share with you is comforting now. There are a number of places we are assured that Jesus Christ of Naza-reth/Messiah Yeshua—the eternal living Lord of all creation—shall return to this Earth and there will be NO mistaking Him when this occurs. It is written that EVERY EYE shall see Him. How that will happen is a mystery, but it will happen nonetheless. The troubles in this world today appear insurmountable, however all things are possible with God and He has provided the way for us to overcome the world through Christ. Paul endured many things, but the Lord delivered him out of all of them. And He will do the same for us.

2 Timothy 3:11 *"Persecutions, afflictions, which came unto me at Antioch, at Iconium, at Lystra; what persecutions I endured: but out of them all the Lord delivered me."*

Revelation 19 clearly gives us some details on the visible return of the Lord Jesus as well as we are instructed to prepare ourselves in Matthew 24. Throughout Philippians 3, Titus, James, and 1 John 3, we find similar information about the visible return of the Messiah and how true believers will be caught up and given glorified indestructible immortal bodies and be with the Lord Jesus forever!

The apostle John wrote in 1 John 3:2, *"Beloved, now are we the sons of God, and it doth not yet appear what we shall be: but we know that, when he shall appear, we shall be like him; for we shall see him as he is. 3 And every man that hath this hope in him purifieth himself, even as he is pure."*

In other words, the Lord created us in His image and likeness to be similar to Jesus so that Jesus can be glorified through the life that we live. When the Lord reappears, we who belong to Him shall become like him, so everyone who has this hope in them as a true born again Spirit-filled Christian believer and disciple ought to be practicing holiness and purifying himself now. Getting into the Word of God so the Word of God gets into you. John also wrote that the testimony of Jesus is the spirit of prophecy.

Revelation 19:10 *"And I fell at his feet to worship him. And he said unto me, See thou do it not: I am thy fellow-servant, and of thy brethren that have the testimony of Jesus: worship God: for the testimony of Jesus is the spirit of prophecy."*

When the resurrected Lord Jesus appeared to the Apostles and the infamous doubting Thomas, Jesus simply appeared in the room and interacted with them as well as eating fish and honeycomb. The Lord Jesus certainly doesn't need a space ship to travel about and there is not a single Holy Scripture that indicates such an idea or concept. When the Lord Jesus returns to this Earth, He will return just as He says He will. Because God means what He said and He said what He means! Just as the angel revealed to us in Acts 1:11 saying, *"Which also said, Ye men of Galilee, why stand ye gazing up into heaven? this same Jesus, which is taken up from you into heaven, shall so come in like manner as ye have seen him go into heaven."*

Just as 2 Thessalonians 1 tells us when the Lord Jesus returns He returns in glory and power. Does it even make sense why anyone or any entity would travel from millions of light years away simply to come to Earth to try to convince us that our Instructional Manual to the Supernatural, known as the Holy Bible, is invalid—that Jesus Christ of Nazareth is not who He claims to be? Think about it. The Bible warned us about this sort of thing happening in the last days.

Mark 13:21-23 *"And then if any man shall say to you, Lo, here is Christ; or, lo, he is there; believe him not: [22]For false Christs and false prophets shall rise, and shall shew signs and wonders, to seduce, if it were possible, even the elect. [23]But take ye heed: behold, I have foretold you all things."*

Chapter Four

GIANTS, FALLEN ANGELS AND EVIL SPIRITS

Before we begin to unravel as much as we are able here, let me first establish that fallen angels are not extraterrestrials or demons. According to the Holy Scriptures, the fallen angels appear to be held in chains of darkness, cast into hell already where they are awaiting the final judgment.

2 Peter 2:4 *"For if God spared not the angels that sinned, but cast them down to hell, and delivered them into chains of darkness, to be reserved unto judgment;"*

We also read in Jude 1:6 *"And the angels which kept not their first estate, but left their own habitation, he hath reserved in everlasting chains under darkness unto the judgment of the great day."*

Angels were not created with physical bodies, although they are very powerful and can take on the appearance of men when the occasion calls for it. How else could some of us "entertain angels unawares" as we read in Hebrews 13:1-2? *"Let brotherly love continue. Be not forgetful to entertain strangers: for thereby some have entertained angels unawares."*

Interestingly, angels can appear in the dazzling white of their glory as we read in Matthew 28:1-3, *"In the end of the sabbath, as it began to dawn toward the first day of the week, came Mary Magdalene and the other Mary to see the sepulchre. 2And, behold, there was a great earthquake: for the angel of the Lord descended from heaven, and came and rolled back the stone from the door, and sat upon it. 3His countenance was like lightning, and his raiment white as snow."* Angels are essentially "ministering spirits," as confirmed in Hebrews 1:14 that says, *"Are they not all ministering spirits, sent forth to minister for them who shall be heirs of salvation?"*

I submit for your consideration that the resurrected Lord Jesus/Yeshua declared in Luke 24:39: *"A spirit hath not flesh and bones, as ye see me have."*

Luke 24:36-44 *"And as they thus spake, Jesus himself stood in the midst of them, and saith unto them, Peace be unto you. ³⁷But they were terrified and affrighted, and supposed that they had seen a spirit. ³⁸And he said unto them, Why are ye troubled? and why do thoughts arise in your hearts? ³⁹Behold my hands and my feet, that it is I myself: handle me, and see; for a spirit hath not flesh and bones, as ye see me have. ⁴⁰And when he had thus spoken, he shewed them his hands and his feet. ⁴¹And while they yet believed not for joy, and wondered, he said unto them, Have ye here any meat? ⁴²And they gave him a piece of a broiled fish, and of an honeycomb.⁴³And he took it, and did eat before them."*

It could very well be that demons are the spirits of those who existed in the world before Adam. This comes out of what some have labeled the "gap theory," because it is based on the gap between Genesis 1:1 and 1:2. Simply stated, there was a world that existed before Adam whose inhabitants so evil God destroyed it and started over. The spirits of these evil beings did not die and they are unable to express their evil natures except through a person or animal. They are the unclean spirits, devils or demons that Jesus cast out.

"When the unclean spirit is gone out of a man, he walketh through dry places, seeking rest; and finding none, he saith, I will return unto my house whence I came out" (Luke 11:24).

When cast out of a man, they appear to be quite tormented and in a dry place. Therefore, they look for a way back in. It is our sin that gives them permission to come in and find rest—which is torment for us.

One of the first things the resurrected Lord Jesus told us is to cast out evil spirits in the authority of His all-powerful name. So it does seem rather curious to me why so few churches teach about these things and help equip their members so healing and restoration will happen.

Mark 16:17 *"And these signs shall follow them that believe; In my name shall they cast out devils; they shall speak with new tongues;"*

Jeremiah 4:23-27 seems to point to this pre-adamic race of beings. *"I beheld the earth, and, lo, it was without form, and void; and the heavens, and they had no light. ²⁴I beheld the mountains, and, lo, they trembled, and all the hills moved lightly. ²⁵I beheld, and, lo, there was no man, and all the birds of the heavens were fled. ²⁶I beheld, and, lo, the fruitful place was a wilderness, and all the cities thereof were broken down at the presence of the LORD, and by his fierce anger. ²⁷For thus hath the LORD said, The whole land shall be desolate; yet will I not make a full end."*

After the great rebellion, they were judged and have possibly become the disembodied invisible evil spirits we battle. Again, we must understand there is an actual war going on in the spiritual world that we must deal with in this physical world.

Ephesians 6:10-12 *"Finally, my brethren, be strong in the Lord, and in the power of his might. ¹¹Put on the whole armour of God, that ye may be able to stand against the wiles of the devil. ¹²For we wrestle not against flesh and blood, but against principalities, against powers, against the rulers of the darkness of this world, against spiritual wickedness in high places."*

As a minister of the gospel of Christ, I have taught and preached for years that these invisible beings desperately want a body to manifest their evil nature through. So if they can, they will find a way to tempt you into agreeing to allow them access in your body. The process starts in your thought life with the enemy tempting you to sin. That's why we must guard our hearts and resist committing participating with evil. Luke 6:45 "A good man out of the good treasure of his heart bringeth forth that which is good; and an evil man out of the evil treasure of his heart bringeth forth that which is evil: for of the abundance of the heart his mouth speaketh."

If you, by your sin, have given unclean spirits access to your spirit, you need to repent and cast them out. Otherwise, they may set up strongholds in your thought life and cause you to be stuck in a pattern of sin.

Keep in mind that these evil invisible disembodied entities also manifest as principalities over entire town, cities, nations and governments. I believe the evidence is proving that all these unclean evil spirits are also able to manifest also as "extraterrestrial aliens," "ghosts" and everything in between.

Now, back to Nephilim. Did you know there is evidence of their existence on this planet? In fact, physical remains have been discovered in places like Peru that appear to be Nephilim skulls and bones. (See Marzulli's books, On the Trail of the Nephilim, and Further Evidence.)

Have you ever noticed that the so-called cavemen of the Ice Age do not fit properly into the Holy Scriptures? However, they do appear to fit in perfectly with this concept of Nephilim. Is it possible that Neanderthal and Nephilim are one and the same? I have seen some very compelling scientific arguments that suggest this is so.

There are numerous accounts of giant skeletons averaging 10 to 30 feet tall discovered in various places and archeological digs. Many finds were written about in newspapers and magazines in the 1700s, 1800s, and early 1900s. This all stopped when certain government agencies, secret societies, or shadow governments decided to hide such evidence because it challenged the theory of Darwinism. In America it appears the Smithsonian played a significant part in all of this.

There are also accounts in diaries and letters going back all the way to the days of Flavius Josephus. He was Born in 34 AD and is considered to be a great Jewish historian. Josephus wrote about the miracles of Jesus Christ, His crucifixion and resurrection, and also believed that Nephilim were the offspring of human women and fallen angels.

In 1856, workers in the Neander Valley near Duesseldorf, Germany, uncovered a skull and bones unlike anything seen before. Upon examination, the skull clearly showed a flattened cranium with a heavy ridge above very large eye sockets. Workers also uncovered an assortment of rather thick and heavily fossilized bones. In the years that succeeded, additional specimens were found in France, Italy, Iraq, and Israel. As far as I am able to ascertain, there are numerous cases of such anomalies all over the world. Some remains do not appear to be 100 percent human. These specimens have been dated to be 13,000 years old and have different DNA than humans.

Isn't it amazing to think that thousands of years ago the Lord had a plan for you to be here for such a time as this!

Jeremiah 1:5 *"Before I formed thee in the belly I knew thee; and before thou camest forth out of the womb I sanctified thee, and I ordained thee a prophet unto the nations."*

Deceptions in World Governments

The governments in America, Russia, China and the UK today, like most all earthly governments, want to stay in control. It appears they are desperately trying to distract us from what they are really doing, sort of like a magician working over an audience with sleight of hand techniques. Misdirection is helpful tool for those who wish to manipulate. Governments may be using misdirection on their citizenry, hoping they will fail to notice the changes taking place.

As difficult as it is to think that our own government may be working behind the scenes to gain greater power, it's important to share with you some of the projects now underway. Let's start with FEMA, the Federal Emergency Management Association. Are you aware that FEMA camps have been set up in every state in America? Their existence has caused rumours that one day the U.S. government will use the occasion of a nation disaster—either accidental or orchestrated—to impose martial law. Some have pointed to the fairly recent government purchases of thousands of guillotines to posit they will be used to dispose of dissidents or even Christians. In fact, martial law was instituted following the Boston Marathon bombing, and the Constitution was suspended while the suspects were tracked down.

Another cause for concern is the government grab for intelligence on U. S. citizens through 24hour surveillance technologies. As we are reaching the end of the age seems not too many people have taken notice of the new laws that have been passed under their noses. The "President's Surveillance Program" was implemented by George W. Bush following the attacks on September 11, 2001. Various whistle-blowers have exposed this classified program which allows domestic spying of Americans through phone calls. It does not require any judicial oversight. The Patriot Act allows the U. S. government to deter and punish terrorists and allows secret searches of homes and businesses and the search of telephone, email and financial records without a court order. In June, 2015, the USA Freedom Act restored and renewed the Patriot Act through 2019. However, it was amended to stop the NSA from continuing its mass phone data collection program.

Chicago Mayor Rahm Emmanuel and former Chief of Staff to President Obama once said, "You never let a serious crisis go to waste." What does that mean? It means they use crisis as a way to continue working their agenda. What is that agenda you may ask? To control mankind. For those who don't trust the government, these types of actions by our elected officials add fuel to the fire.

How will the world handle information about extraterrestrials if they reject their true identity of demons? I recall a speech that shocked the audience at the University of Toronto in September 25, 2005. It certainly caught the attention of the mainstream media. Paul Hellyer, former Defense Minister of Canada, made headlines by publicly announcing that he believes UFOs are real. He was quoted as saying, "We lived too long in a sense of isolation, thinking that Earth was the center of the cosmos, that we were the only species, and, therefore, probably the most advanced." Hellyer also shared this idea at the 2013 "Citizen Hearing on Disclosure" before the U. S. Congress and on Russian television when he appeared on the program Sophie Co.

Hellyer gives credence to the UFO phenomena and has helped changed the attitudes of scoffers, doubters and unbelievers who previously wrote these things off as conspiracy theories. My favorite quote from his is that, "UFOs are as real as the airplanes that fly over your head." Hellyer also declared that aliens walk amongst us and are responsible for such modern advances as the microchip, LED light, and Kevlar vest. May I submit to you that perhaps these devils who have been around from before the time of man took human women in exchange for technology, according to the account in Genesis 6:4?

Hellyer has also stated, "[I've] been getting from various sources [that] there are about 80 different species and some of them look just like us and they could walk down the street and you wouldn't know if you walked past one."

Now, while believes that these Hellyer beings from outer space have arrived here from the Pleiades and Zeta Reticuli star systems, and through a portal in the Andes Mountains, I believe these are simply the manifestations of demons, taking on whatever form they choose.

Another strange program is HAARP, which stands for High Frequency Active Auroral Research Program. This team of government approved and paid for researchers conduct experiments which use electromagnetic frequencies to fire pulsed, directed energy beams. The beams "temporarily excite a limited area of the ionosphere," according to the HAARP website. Some of those same researchers are concerned that these disturbances could have major consequences, causing tsunamis and earthquakes.

God's Promise of Peace

For all those called to Christ's plan and purpose we have this amazing promise.

1 Corinthians 2:9 *"But as it is written, Eye hath not seen, nor ear heard, neither have entered into the heart of man, the things which God hath prepared for them that love him."*

I hope by what you have read so far that you have gained more understanding. I must assume you are seeking the whole truth and nothing but the truth. Let us therefore continue to pray in the almighty name of Jesus for all those who still need to make their peace with the Lord. Let's stop bowing down to the spirit of fear, which is the opposite of faith—and without faith it is impossible to please the Lord.

"But without faith it is impossible to please him: for he that cometh to God must believe that he is, and that he is a rewarder of them that diligently seek him" (Hebrews 11:6).

In John 13:34, the Lord Jesus/Yeshua gave us a commandment to love one another as He loves us. That surely means helping people find the narrow pathway to salvation. Matthew 7:14 says, *"Because strait is the gate, and narrow is the way, which leadeth unto life, and few there be that find it."*

To truly love means I will not endorse lies, but rather help you recognize them. Our goals is, *"To open their eyes, and to turn them from darkness to light, and from the power of Satan unto God, that they may receive forgiveness of sins, and inheritance among them which are sanctified by faith that is in me"* (Acts 26:18).

Chapter Five

TRANSHUMANISM, GOVERNMENT SECRETS, CERN AND STRANGE VISIONS

More bells and whistles, with glitter and gold,

More motivational slick speakers just as the prophets
had foretold

More programs with singles' groups
checking each other out

Dating and entertaining spirits of unbelief and doubt

Political correctness equals not telling the truth

See how it is orchestrated to indoctrinate the youth?

More empire buildings with seeker-sensitive words

Why are so few willing to be biblical scholarly nerds?

With no supernatural power of the Gospel being displayed,

Let those who know the truth continually pray

If you worship the Lord in Spirit and in Truth
then let it be known that Jesus is forever almighty
upon His throne, therefore you are not alone

So share Christ's love by doing the same

Heal the sick and cast out demons in the authority
of His all powerful Name.

Caspar McCloud (c) 2014

2 Timothy 3:5 *"Having a form of godliness, but denying the power thereof: from such turn away."*

I watched evangelist Reinhard Bonnke, one of my heroes of the faith, present a New Year's Eve message in 2014 at a youth conference. As soon as he walked onto the platform and stood before the gathering I felt the atmosphere in the room dramatically change. He shared in humbleness how the Lord gave him a vision for Africa many years ago when he was seeing very little fruit from all his efforts to help lead people into salvation. He spoke wonderful, encouraging words and testified that he has now seen more than 75 million people, mostly from Africa, become born-again Christians. He shared how the Lord has now moved him to America and he boldly and emotionally proclaimed, "America shall be saved," which brought the crowd to their feet with thunderous applause.

This begs the question, under what circumstances shall America be saved? How often does someone receive salvation and experience being born-again without realising how desperately lost they were without the Lord? After 9/11 most churches were packed out with people seeking spiritual, emotional, and physical resolution from the tragedy. Where are they today? Just because we haven't had a tragedy of similar size doesn't mean it won't happen again.

There are a number of prophetic warnings about impending disasters. Prophets like A. A. Allen had a vision July 4, 1954, of widespread desolation brought about by terrific explosions from the Atlantic to the Pacific ocean. My Native American friend, Chief Joseph Riverwind, confirms this, saying he has heard from God that the fires will soon come upon us.

Gene Splicing

Scientists today use an inexpensive tool called a CRISPR to edit genes. The CRISPR allows them to edit genomes with unprecedented precision, efficiency and flexibility. New creations include monkeys with targeted mutations and the ability to prevent HIV infection in human cells. Chinese scientists claim to have used the technique on nonviable human embryos. How long do you think it will be before "designer babies" are commonplace?

We are already experiencing the results of modified genes in food crops. Ninety percent of the corn and soy that are grown in the U. S. have been genetically modified, and the debate continues on whether this is harmful or benign. What are the chances some will misuse these abilities to create things that ought not be?

There is something new in neuroscience called optogenetics. With invasive surgery, scientists have discovered ways to basically turn on or off switches in your brain to supposedly treat conditions of people suffering from things like depression or chronic pain. Science may think this is an easy solution but to me it seems rather a form of control and witchcraft. What would stop someone from using this process for evil? Those of us who understand ancient prophesy may actually be hindering the New World Order.

The Scriptures tell us about a spirit of heaviness and how our thought life plays a major role in all this. Thus second Corinthians 10:5 says we are to take every thought captive to the obedience of Christ.

The transhumanists have ideas that I am sure aren't from their own original thoughts about how they may improve upon God's divine creation. They are eager to explore the possibilities! Giant steps have been made in the last few years in such fields as artificial intelligence, robotics, genetics, nanotechnology, and cybernetics. Most of the scientists working in these areas have been programmed by a Darwinian mind-set and often ignorantly embrace atheism. They hope to find ways to live forever without the Lord.

Gene editing actually has enormous potential to fulfill the dreams of what the early eugenics movement tried to do. Modern eugenics began in the early 20th century with the seemingly noble objective of improving one's genetic stock by encouraging certain "fit" individuals to reproduce, and dissuading other deemed "unfit." The unfit included people with mental or physical disabilities, had low IQs and were members of minorities. The eugenic movement was pursued in Nazi Germany and by Americans such as Margaret Sanger, who is the founder of the abortion movement. Would it surprise you to learn that today abortion is the leading cause of death in the African Americans community?

Genesis 6 refers to some sort of incursion that altered man's DNA. Did demons or fallen angels conduct gene splicing, or use supernatural methods to contaminate the entire human race that only Noah and his family remained pure from the lineage of Adam? I dare say the evidence is mounting that the same unclean spirits that showed up in Noah's day are manifesting again today. As a result, people are submitting to a similar pathway of thinking that shall ultimately lead to their destruction and death.

I have shared with my church fellowship numerous times and in conferences how we really must stop putting limits on how the Lord might fix things in this broken world. Consider this: Fleas are tiny insects, yet quite accomplished at jumping great distances. If a human could actually jump like a flea, we could leap more than 900 feet into the air! It reminds me of that old film about the absent minded professor who invented the antigravity substance he called "flubber." Despite the fleas' amazing jumping ability, the Creator designed them so they can be easily trained to limit themselves—simply by putting a lid on their environment. In just three days, they will learn that it is quite futile to jump as high as their God given potential. So that when the lid is removed, they won't jump any higher than the top of the jar. Research reveals the fleas offspring will also inherent these limitations. This is an example of transgenerational epigenetic inheritance: something invisible is influencing thoughts and expressions that are being passed on generationally (see Numbers 14:18).

Perhaps you feel like you have been knocking up against some invisible "lids" placed over your life. Have you been taught to limit yourself? Or have you gotten the limitations generationally? After all, God almighty is without limits. Why not begin to take the spiritual lid off of your thinking today, and perhaps you may learn to jump 900 feet or even higher!

Mark 11:24 *"Therefore I say unto you, What things soever ye desire, when ye pray, believe that ye receive them, and ye shall have them."*

John 14:13 "And whatsoever ye shall ask in my name, that will I do, that the Father may be glorified in the Son."

We all go through times of difficulties in this fallen world; however, we must always keep in mind as true believers, the power of the Holy Spirit in us is greater than any spirit that would come against us! The same Holy Spirit that resurrected the Lord Jesus/Yeshua out of that tomb has no limits. Sometimes it is our stinking thinking and lack of knowledge of the Word that limits the power of God.

There are biochemical changes that occur during any stressful event you encounter, which may have significant short and long term impact on your brain. That in turn can affect our reasoning abilities, our memory and emotions. Best to stay in God's Word all the time and enjoy His supernatural peace. Philippians 4:7, *"And the peace of God, which passeth all understanding, shall keep your hearts and minds through Christ Jesus."*

Now it is interesting to me how people perceive information and how they process this to understand the world. Genetics plays a hand into all this, as the Bible says the sins of the father are passed on to the third and fourth generations. We know that our experiences help colour our perceptions, and all of us deal with generational blessings and curses this side of heaven.

The word "generation" contains the root word "gene." A gene is a basic unit of heredity capable of transmitting characteristics from one generation to the next. It consists of a specific sequence of DNA or RNA that occupies a fixed position on a chromosome. RNA is short for Ribonucleic acid and consists of many layers, each with their own unique roles. Collectively, they perform multiple vital roles in coding, decoding, regulation, and giving expression to the genes.

Did you know that generational blessings or curses can be attached to the genes you inherited from you ancestors?

A spirit of fear, that God did not give you, may have been established in your generations all the way back to Adam. It became a stronghold in your DNA, which makes fear feel like it's a part of your personality. What if you were able to break that off in the name of Jesus Christ of Nazareth? Just repenting for allowing fear to be greater than faith in God in your generations can be the key to a new life of hope and peace.

The transmittance of genetic code from one generation to another is called 'transgenerational epigenetic inheritance.' Scientists are finding that something invisible outside the cell appears to be influencing it and altering things by turning on and off certain controls and switches on the genes. It is my personal opinion this is the work of invisible creatures of darkness. Repentance for believing their lies and acting upon them is what God will use to free us and alter those genes.

Do you think I am a wee bit too serious about the things of God? Here's what the Scripture says, *"Draw nigh to God, and he will draw nigh to you. Cleanse your hands, ye sinners; and purify your hearts, ye double minded"* (James 4:8).

"Set your affection on things above, not on things on the earth" (Colossians 3:2).

U.S. Government's Report on Aliens

In 2011, certain important documents written by FBI agents in 1947 were released and declassified so that the public is now allowed to view them. These reports supposedly present clear evidence that we have been visited by extraterrestrial beings from an ethereal plane coexistent somewhere within our physical universe. These beings are said to materialize at will as translucent figures. It sounds to me like 2 Corinthians 11:14, *"And no marvel; for Satan himself is transformed into an angel of light."*

Here is a summary of the reports of the aliens and their space ships (disks).

1. Part of the disks carry crews, others are under remote control

2. Their mission is peaceful. The visitors contemplate settling on this plane

3. These visitors are humanlike but much larger in size

4. They are not excarnate Earth people, but come from their own world

5. They do NOT come from a planet as we use the word, but from an etheric planet which interpenetrates with our own and is not perceptible to us

6. The bodies of the visitors, and the craft, automatically materialize on entering the vibratory rate of our dense matter

7. The disks posses a type of radiant energy or a ray, which will easily disintegrate any attacking ship. They reenter the

etheric at will, and so simply disappear from our vision, without trace

8. The region from which they come is not the "astral plane," but corresponds to the Lokas or Talas. Students of esoteric matters will understand these terms.

9. They probably can not be reached by radio, but probably can be by radar if a signal system can be devised for that (apparatus)

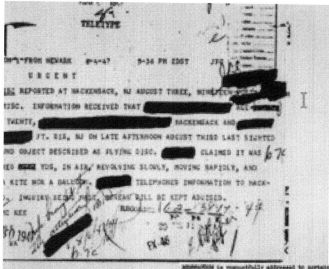

Actual documentation
from the FBI

Now I ask you, did these beings come from other planets and other dimensions, or is it more likely that they were demons and those agents were duped?

This sounds to me very like the apparitions of the Virgin Mary that appeared in various places throughout the world. More than 40 million people have visited Medjugorje, Yugoslavia since the apparitions began in 1981. Other apparitions have manifested in Lourdes, France and Fatima, Portugal.

Back in the 80's I had a meeting with the editor of a newspaper who happened to be of the Catholic faith and had travelled to Medjugorje to experience things for himself. He gave me a list of things the Virgin Mary said, and as I recall, each statement sounded nice but also went against the Holy Scriptures.

When this editor told me he believed the Virgin Mary apparition was genuine. One of the things she said was that all religions lead to God. I asked him why then did Jesus/Yeshua say: John 14:6, *"Jesus saith unto him, I am the way, the truth, and the life: no man cometh unto the Father, but by me."*

The editor was most uncomfortable!

True revivals throughout history represent a genuine move of the Holy Spirit that brings repentance where people are forever changed from the inside out. They are truly transformed, have a closer walk with the Lord, and have signs, wonders, healing, and miracles following. The presence of God comes in such a way that it ignites in us a spiritual inner fire with the dunamis power of the Lord. (This where we get our modern term "dynamite.") It blows apart the old ways and brings in the new.

Today we have numerous believers who have not been taught to interpret prophecy properly, so they believe that when the Scriptures says things like *"But evil men and seducers shall wax worse and worse, deceiving, and being deceived,"* (2 Timothy 3:13), we can do nothing to change it. I dare say we are still in a season, prophetically speaking, where Papa God is still extending His mercy, grace and love and is more than willing and able to answer our prayers when we meet His requirements. This does not go contrary to prophecy, as all things are possible with God (see Matthew 19:26, Luke 1:37, Mark 10:27).

Even as evildoers continually grow worse as they embrace immorality and great spiritual deception, God's remnant church is still making a difference. It shall never fail, generation after generation, until it has fulfilled its mission on earth as Jesus/Yeshua has commanded. He had not yet established His church when he said, *"And I say also unto thee, That thou art Peter, and upon this rock I will build my church, and the gates of hell shall not prevail against it"* (Matthew 16:18). The word "church" used here is derived from the Greek *ekklasia*, which means the "called out" or "assembly." We shall all be assembled together with Christ when we are caught up together and what a day that shall be!

These are indeed unprecedented times and the Church cannot really ignore these issues if we are going to be overcomers and soul winners. Secular people are attracted to investigating these sorts of bizarre accounts, and many are figuring out that there has been a deliberate suppression of the true history of the world. So they want to know about such things as the Stargates or open portals which the Bible reveals through the story of Jacob's ladder. Might we ask who really built the pyramids—was it Nephilim? Are those ancient accounts of places like Atlantis true? If we don't provide answers, the secularists will, as they are already doing on such shows as Ancient Aliens where they are obviously trying to alter and discredit Biblical history.

Some of the most recent theories about intergalactic transportation system have to do with black holes. Scientists say black holes are places in space that have gravitational fields so intense, no matter or radiation can escape. Any matter entering the event horizon, which is a theoretical boundary around a black hole, is added to its mass. Two examples of the event horizon are the transfiguration (see Matthew 17) and the resurrection. At both events, Christ was between dimensions, as it were.

CERN's Hadron Collider

I think the development of the Large Hadron Collider (LHC) at the CERN laboratory, near Geneva, Switzerland, is one of the most serious events happening in the world today. If you haven't heard of it, you're not alone. The media keeps the world busy looking at the sideshow while the critical stories go unreported. The collider is a particle accelerator that causes protons to travel at very high speeds in opposite directions so that they collide with each other. This creates an enormous burst of energy. Scientists ultimately hope to discover the secrets of the creation of the universe which many believe to have happened billions of years ago. They are also working on a device that can bend space and time to open dimensional portals or Stargates—in order to travel to other dimensions and times.

Many bizarre accounts or paranormal activity have been shared or leaked describing what is happening in restricted areas of CERN. The world seems overwhelmed with information and disinformation such that a spirit of confusion reigns. 1 Corinthians 14:33, *"For God is not the author of confusion, but of peace, as in all churches of the saints."*

History is full of strange accounts of the gods and goddess of false religions travelling from one location to another using some sort of machinery (UFO) that would allow them to traverse dimensions.

Keep in mind that with God almighty, there is no need for such artificial means. Remember the account of Philip and the eunuch? The Spirit of the Lord caught Philip away, such that the eunuch saw him no more (Acts 8:3839). In 2 Kings 2:11, Elijah went up to heaven by a whirlwind. In the New Testament, the resurrected Jesus/Yeshua is able to suddenly appear inside a room.

John 20:26 *"And after eight days again his disciples were within, and Thomas with them: then came to Jesus, the doors being shut, and stood in the midst, and said, Peace be unto you."*

Was it possible that in the period before the flood of Noah the ancients were able to travel through time? There are several accounts of the ancient Sumerian so-called gods and goddess coming in through open stargates, as represented on carvings and other ancient artwork. I suggest the capability was taught to them by the fallen angels. Could the same evil spirits be giving the same understanding to the scientists at CERN today?

CERN officials have gone on record saying that they want to open a gateway into another dimension and find God. Is it merely a coincidence that CERN (the European Organization for Nuclear Research) is also short for the horned god Cernunnos, the god of the underworld? The Large Hadron Collider in Switzerland is miles underground. Cernunnos was the horned deity of the Celts/Gauls later referred to as Pan. (See pictures section of this book.)

Jude 1:6, *"And the angels which kept not their first estate, but left their own habitation, he hath reserved in everlasting chains under darkness unto the judgment of the great day."*

Sergio Bertolucci, Director for Research and Scientific Computing at CERN is quoted as saying: "Something may come through dimensional 'doors' at LHC... Or we might send something through it."

Is CERN a key location for such entities to like Cernunnos to reemerge? We could also call him Pan or Saturn, or by his most familiar name, Satan. Is this where his demonic army will manifest openly in our dimension? Is this the open door to hell and the bottomless pit?

Scripture reveals this is part of a plan for the elite's agenda to usher in their New World Order of one world government and religious system. Those who read this and say to themselves, "This is all nonsense; I don't believe any of this," may be fulfilling 2 Peter 3:3-9

"Knowing this first, that there shall come in the last days scoffers, walking after their own lusts, ⁴And saying, Where is the promise of his coming? for since the fathers fell asleep, all things continue as they were from the beginning of the creation. ⁵For this, they willingly are ignorant of, that by the word of God the heavens were of old, and the earth standing out of the water and in the water: ⁶Whereby the world that then was, being overflowed with water, perished: ⁷But the heavens and the earth, which are now, by the same word are kept in store, reserved unto fire against the day of judgment and perdition of ungodly men. ⁸But, beloved, be not ignorant of this one thing, that one day is with the Lord as a thousand years and a thousand years as one day. ⁹The Lord is not slack concerning his promise, as some men count slackness; but is longsuffering to usward, not willing that any should perish, but that all should come to repentance.

We, the Church, really need to be prepared and understand!

Throughout the Holy Scriptures we are confronted with the supernatural, and that makes it even more intriguing how videos and photos have confirmed this concept. If you go to the internet, you can find photos of the Norway spiral, which was a spinning light in the night sky over Norway and like nothing ever seen before. It certainly does make one question reality as we once knew it.

The Strange Location of CERN

CERN was built over an area called "Saint Genis Pouilly;" the name Pouilly appears to come from the Latin "Appolliacum." Many scholars believe that in Roman times there was a temple honouring Apollo on this same spot. What's more, for centuries the local residents have believed it was and is an open portal, or gateway, to the underworld. This sounds to me like Apollyon in Greek, and Abbadon in Hebrew, the bottomless pit described in Revelation.

Revelation 9:12 *"And the fifth angel sounded, and I saw a star fall from heaven unto the earth: and to him was given the key of the bottomless pit. And he opened the bottomless pit; and there arose a smoke out of the pit, as the smoke of a great furnace; and the sun and the air were darkened by reason of the smoke of the pit."*

Revelation 9:11 *"And they had a king over them, which is the angel of the bottomless pit, whose name in the Hebrew tongue is Abaddon, but in the Greek tongue hath his name Apollyon."*

Revelation 11:7 *"And when they shall have finished their testimony, the beast that ascendeth out of the bottomless pit shall make war against them, and shall overcome them, and kill them."*

Until recently, corporations would shun being connected with any religious or spiritual interest. However, the powers that be at CERN actually chose to flaunt Shiva, a Hindu goddess as a symbolic mascot outside its headquarters. This is also Apollyon, known as the goddess of destruction. Perhaps the powers behind the New World Order are sending a message hidden in plain sight. Is it possible they are attempting to use the LHC to open a gateway to the bottomless pit?

Revelation 13:11-12 *"And I beheld another beast coming up out of the earth, and he had two horns like a lamb, and he spake as a dragon. And he exerciseth all the power of the first beast before him and causeth the earth and them which dwell therein to worship the first beast whose deadly wound was healed."*

Modern day Israel is still looking for the Messiah who will sit in a new temple as king and bring world peace. They are ignorant of the Holy Scriptures that tell us the Antichrist shall do this. The devil is doing his best to frighten and discourage everyone; however, we are still instructed in Matthew 28:19-20, *"Go ye therefore, and teach all nations, baptizing them in the name of the Father, and of the Son, and of the Holy Ghost: Teaching them to observe all things whatsoever I have commanded you: and, lo, I am with you always, even unto the end of the world. Amen."*

Who can you encourage and share Christ's love with today? Be encouraged, even though most people won't attend church with you, they will listen to someone who walks in Christ's love and sincerely respects them. So share Christ's love any way you can and bless them anyway you are able. After all the Lord Jesus told us in John 4:35, *"Say not ye, There are yet four months, and then cometh harvest? behold, I say unto you, Lift up your eyes, and look on the fields; for they are white already to harvest."*

There have been a numbers of times I have prayed and ministered to an unbeliever who needed healing and restoration. I have moved in the supernatural confidence of the Holy Spirit that my faith shall trump their unbelief. Many were healed and came face-to-face with the awesome love and almighty power of the Lord Jesus. Many were soon converted when they realised the gospel is absolutely true. Scripture instructs us that there is always someone who is ready to get saved because all things are possible with God as He would none be lost!

Simplicity of the Gospel vs. the Great Deception

While a youth, I came to understand the simplicity of the gospel, which helped ground me from the beginning. The simplicity is that Jesus Christ of Nazareth is physically, eternally and supernaturally alive today; that He is soon returning to take over this entire world; and that He died on that cross and rose from the dead on the third day making a way possible that we who believe and obey His commandments can live with Him forever. How can this not be the most vitally important event in all of history?

From that foundation, it is now built into my DNA to keep extending Christ's mercy, grace and love to all. I have ministered to many over the years who shared with me how they have been wounded in their life by things like parents letting them down, friends who betrayed them, hurt through divorce and struggles with drugs and alcohol. Many tell me how their church let them down, how they are fearful of the future and ashamed of their past. Most all addictions and murmuring and complaining are simply a result of not feeling loved. Not being connected with the awesome love of God. I have also ministered to people who have claimed to have been abducted by these so-called extraterrestrials, and even have substantial evidence to back up their claims. Suffice to say, the power of the Blood of Jesus still covers all sins and all troubles when we appropriate the finished work of the cross.

Today we are watching Satan unleash his end-time delusions with lying signs and wonders. Many of the New Age ideas that only a few years ago seemed totally ridiculous have now managed to make inroads into the mainstream media. Their philosophy has become the new normal, perhaps preparing the way for the New World Order and global sense of enlightenment.

Consider how enamored the mainstream media was just a few years ago with the possibility that the Mayan calendar, which ended in 2012, actually might have predicted the end of the world. This is what I call a red herring, and I recall pointing out during that time that our calendar ends every year.

Why was there so little information shared about the Mayan's practice of sacrificing many thousands of their own people to "Quetzalcoatl," their demonic god? The Mayan people did so to appease their god in hopes of opening the portals for the demons to enter into this dimension and empower them. Do you see a parallel with today's government sanctioned abortions? It makes one wonder if the pro-choice movement is related somehow and they hope to open the same portal to the same demonic force. After all, the Lord tells us in Leviticus 18:21, *"And thou shalt not let any of thy seed pass through the fire to Molech, neither shalt thou profane the name of thy God: I am the LORD."*

Psalm 106:37 *"Yea, they sacrificed their sons and their daughters unto devils,"*

What we were not told about the Mayan prophecy is that they actually said that 2012 would be the end of an era, and a new one—the final dispensation of mankind would begin.

How imminent is the Lord's return? Not before mankind comes under Satanic deception which causes the great falling way to occur.

We already have a one-world government in place called the UN, and its world court is already in session. What is missing is a oneworld religion. How can that happen with so many religions in the world today? Perhaps while we're distracted by the troubles emanating from the Middle East, Islam will complete its world domination and establish Islamic Sharia law (for more on this law go to: http://www.billionbibles.org/sharia/sharialaw.html).

We are warned specifically about the great deception as found in 2 Thessalonians 2:1-13.

¹Now we beseech you, brethren, by the coming of our Lord Jesus Christ, and by our gathering together unto him,"

This refers to the rapture of the church and the second coming of Christ. They are two separate events. The Greek word for rapture is "endoxadzo," which means to adorn with glory, referring to the amazing blessings conferred upon the saints of Christ as joint heirs who will help rule universes. At the rapture, all the dead and all the living who are in Christ will vanish from the earth in a moment, in the twinkling of an eye. Not one soul will be left on earth that is a true Christian.

²That ye be not soon shaken in mind, or be troubled, neither by spirit, nor by word, nor by letter as from us, as that the day of Christ is at hand.

³Let no man deceive you by any means: for that day shall not come, except there come a falling away first, and that man of sin be revealed, the son of perdition;

Preceding this gathering of the Church will be apostasy and the revealing of the Antichrist. One definition of an apostasy is the act of leaving behind, or falling away from, your religious or political beliefs and principles. This is a very serious event that shall have people disregard the truth for a lie.

⁴Who opposeth and exalteth himself above all that is called God, or that is worshipped; so that he as God sitteth in the temple of God, shewing himself that he is God.

This is speaking about the beast that desires to be worshipped.

⁵Remember ye not, that, when I was yet with you, I told you these things?

This is a direct Holy Spirit question, and we can answer, Yes, we have been amply forewarned.

⁶And now ye know what withholdeth that he might be revealed in his time.

⁷For the mystery of iniquity doth already work: only he who now letteth will let, until he be taken out of the way.

What was it the early church knew? What was hindering the mystery of iniquity, or spirit of lawlessness? If they understood this then, shouldn't we understand this now? The Lord is telling us that there will be a time just before Christ's return when some will depart from the faith, giving heed to seducing spirits, giving heed to doctrines of devils, speaking lies in hypocrisy, having their conscience seared with a hot iron, forbidding to marry, commanding to abstain from meats. Take a good look around. Isn't this what we see?

This is most certainly speaking about what life will look like for those who remain after the Church has been caught up with the Lord in the air. What shall happen after the church has disappeared from the whole Earth? Will the governments and false religious leaders tell those who are left behind that the aliens took us because we were standing in the way of the New World Order and its agenda of world peace?

⁸And then shall that Wicked be revealed, whom the Lord shall consume with the spirit of his mouth, and shall destroy with the brightness of his coming:

In other words, the Antichrist would have to come after the church is raptured according to 1 Thessalonians 4:13-16. I don't believe the saints of the Lord Jesus shall be here to experience the tribulations during the shortlived reign of the Antichrist (see Matthew 24:1521, Revelation 6:11,9,21) although some would disagree with me on the timing.

⁹Even him, whose coming is after the working of Satan with all power and signs and lying wonders,

After the working of Satan" means that the beast of the satanic spirit will come out of the abyss to inhabit a human who is the Antichrist.

¹⁰And with all deceivableness of unrighteousness in them that perish; because they received not the love of the truth, that they might be saved. ¹¹And for this cause God shall send them strong delusion, that they should believe a lie:

Every evil practice known to mankind will have been employed to deceive all those who reject the gospel and are destined to perish. This is the great deception, and God will permit it. If someone is destined to go to hell by rejecting the Lord Jesus there is nothing further God can do to rescue them at this point. He cannot go against the truth that all men come to Him only through Jesus Christ. It is not Papa God's will that anyone should perish, but that all should come to repentance.

The Lord has designed and created us with freewill and so if someone persists in staying in rebellion, serving the wrong kingdom, then the Lord God shall allow them to go their own way. God cannot go against His own Word even though it shall damn their soul forever.

¹²That they all might be damned who believed not the truth, but had pleasure in unrighteousness.

It is a choice; we can choose today where we spend eternity.

¹³But we are bound to give thanks always to God for you, brethren beloved of the Lord, because God hath from the beginning chosen you to salvation through sanctification of the Spirit and belief of the truth:

There will be a great falling away when numerous professing Christians will turn away from the faith. The word used in the Greek is apostasia, which basically means backsliding, or falling away. How will professing believers who are attending the feel good tickle my ear churches hold up? It appears that many popular churches today cleverly avoid quoting the Holy Scriptures on the subject of sin and repentance. How shall those who are not grounded in the Word of God cope with strong delusion?

.already warned you about the Pope speaking of baptiz-
aliens and the LUCIFER telescope. Perhaps the Vatican
.aall claim Jesus was genetically engineered by a superiour
advanced civilization and that's why He was able to perform
such healing and miracles and this will help set up the great
falling away and final rebellion.

1 Timothy 4:1 *"Now the Spirit speaketh expressly, that in
the latter times some shall depart from the faith, giving heed to
seducing spirits, and doctrines of devils;"*

As I have shared many times before, I am again reminded of
this very stern warning given in Galatians 1:8, *"But though we,
or an angel from heaven, preach any other gospel unto you than
that which we have preached unto you, let him be accursed."*

One can only speculate how this will exactly play out. Now
is the time to become firmly grounded in the truth and warn
as many as people as possible.

Matthew 24:13 *"But he that shall endure unto the end, the
same shall be saved."*

Matthew 10:22 *"And ye shall be hated of all men for my
name's sake: but he that endureth to the end shall be saved."*

Revelation 3:5 *"He that overcometh, the same shall be clothed
in white raiment; and I will not blot out his name out of the book
of life, but I will confess his name before my Father, and before
his angels."*

Just as the early disciples did when confronted with the
reality of Jesus' crucifixion, we must move out of our disbelief
and into a mind-set that allows us to be prepared for what will
certainly take place.

As things unfold in the future, I pray you are able to discern
and recognise the lying signs and wonders of the great deception. Keep in mind that UFOs and their occupants are not from
some distant galaxy, but rather demonic manifestations from
another dimension. They come only to kill, steal, and destroy.

PICTURES

Historic Judiculla Rock, Jackson County
Styles North Carolina

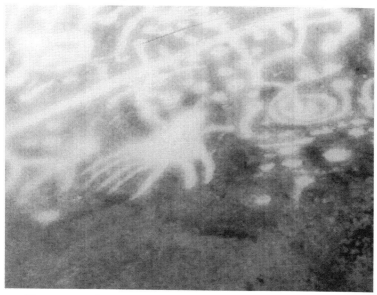

Close up of ancient embedded seven finger hand

First meeting with Riverwinds left side - Chief Joseph
Riverwind, Dr. Lew Davis, Dr. Laralyn Riverwind,
Alice Miller right side - Mark Warren,
L.A. Marzulli, Pastor Caspar McCloud, Sam Miller

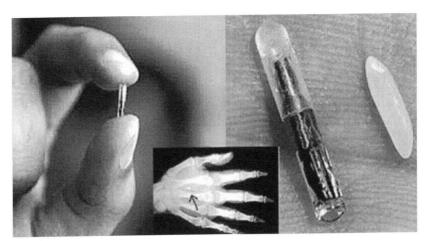

Microchips are a reality and the technology exists today
that at some juncture people shall be compelled to submit to
taking a subcutaneous RFID (Radio-frequency identification)
chip. For what is prophesied in Holy Scriptures
shall come to pass

Author next to rock with ancient pictographs

Sam and Alice Miller, Pastor Caspar McCloud,
and L.A. Marzulli

Demonic figure "Pan"

Pastor McCloud and L A Marzulli on the trail
researching at undisclosed location

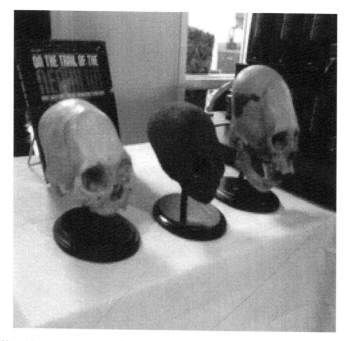

Replications of actual elongated skulls from Peru brought
discovered by Marzulli and Shaw

L.A. Marzulli received
symbolic key to
understanding and
unlocking mysteries. A
gift from Chief Joseph
Riverwind

Baby elongated skull at conference book table with
McCloud and Marzulli

Author with his hand comparing size of embedded ancient
seven finger hand, photograph taken by L.A. Marzulli

Mysterious ancient mounds in North Carolina

Artifact found in ancient
mounds in North Carolina

Georgia guide stones
Photo taken by L.A. Marzulli

Author whilst on research expedition in UK visited Battle
of Britain Museum.

Paul McGuire, Caspar McCloud, L.A. Marzulli

Caspar McCloud and Tom Horn

Author photographed UFO over roof of house the 6th of
November 2014 in North Georgia

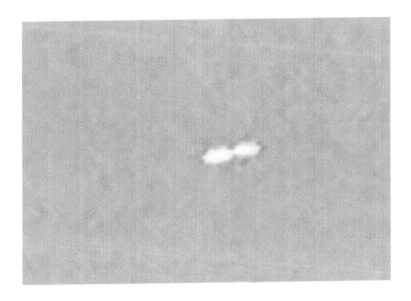

Enlargement of above picture

UFO Photographs by permission of Richard Shaw

UFO Pictures by permission of Richard Shaw

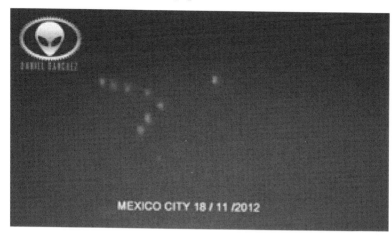

UFO
Fleet

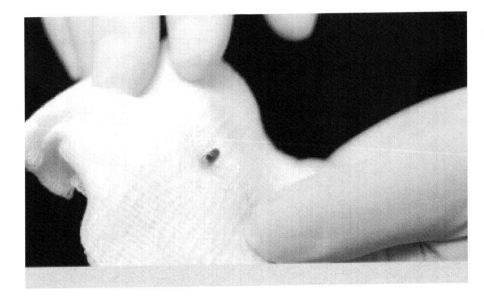

Close up of Implant Removed

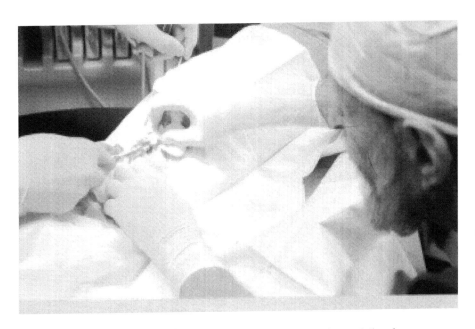

Dr. Roger Leir removing implant, It had vanished as
surgery begun until L. A. Marzulli prayed and it suddenly
re-appeared and was thus surgically taken out of patients leg

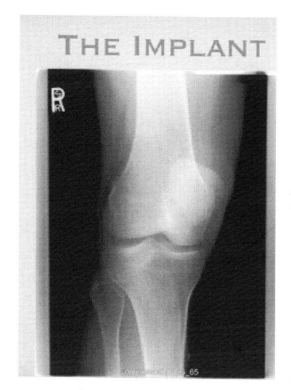

Xray of Alien Implant

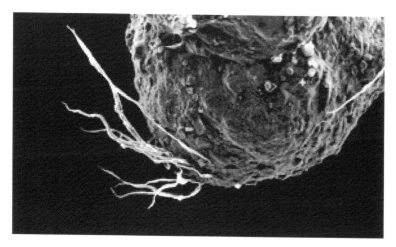

Alien Implant SEM

Chapter Six

THE ILLUMINATI AND THE NEW WORLD ORDER

You may wonder how a nation that was founded on righteousness and biblical truths can have fallen so far. Let's take a little journey to see the actual foundations of our "faith."

The Founding of A Nation

I love reading the stories about the Puritans, or Pilgrims, as they just wanted to obey the Holy Word of God over what anyone else did or said. They went through some rather awful persecution in England, then risked everything to find a new world, free from the doctrines of men and devils interfering. However, did you know that the majority of our Founding Fathers were not, in fact, Christians? Many of them were members of the Freemasons. In fact 44 of the 56 signers of the Declaration of Independence were upper-echelon Freemasons, connected to the European order.

In their "secret book," which can now be ordered online called Morals and Dogmas of Freemasonry by Albert Pike, the Prince of Mercy degree describes a disturbing form of religion that is troubling to Christians. It was written by Pike, but one might say he was directed by an antichrist spirit. If you an unfamiliar with this religion that passes itself off as a "club," the most troubling of the tenets is the belief that Jesus was created by Lucifer, and that Jesus did not come in the flesh, but only appeared to come in the flesh. This heresy that Jesus was created by Lucifer is the foundation for the Illuminati belief that the roles of God and Satan are reversed. They believe that because God made the Tree of the Knowledge of Good and Evil off-limits to Adam and Eve, God is evil and Satan is good.

Let me share something with on page 567 of Pike's: "To deliver the soul captive in darkness the principal of light or genius of the son charged to redeem the intellectual world of that which is the type came to manifest himself amongst men." Presumably, Pike was misquoting and mangling John 1:5, *"And the light shineth in darkness; and the darkness comprehended it not,"* when he wrote the following. "Light appeared in the darkness, but the darkness comprehended it not according to the words of St. John. The light could not unite with the darkness, but put on the appearance of a human body and took the name of Christ and the Messiah only to accommodate itself to the language of the Jews."

The Bible says that any spirit that does not confess that Jesus Christ came in the flesh is a spirit of antichrist.

1 John 4:3 *"And every spirit that confesseth not that Jesus Christ is come in the flesh is not of God: and this is that spirit of antichrist, whereof ye have heard that it should come; and even now already is it in the world."*

In some ways, modern Christianity is now suffering a similar misrepresentation because believers don't understand that the power of God is available to mankind. Jesus/Yeshua divested Himself of the glory he had with the Father; that's why He had to be, in a sense, re-glorified. If you recall, He said, *"Don't touch me,"* to the women who first saw Him outside the tomb. He said it was because He was not yet glorified. John 20:17, *"Jesus saith unto her, Touch me not; for I am not yet ascended to my Father: but go to my brethren, and say unto them, I ascend unto my Father, and your Father; and to my God, and your God."*

After this Jesus/Yeshua could suddenly appear inside a locked room and never walk through a door, He could also eat fish and bread down by the sea with His followers. Now He has given us the same power so we can perform miracles, heal the sick, and cast out devils in His name. We need to undo the programming that says things like, "I can't minister in the name of Jesus healing and deliverance—only Jesus could do that because He was God".

My friend Chief Joseph Riverwind relates that when he was in the U. S. Army doing his best to be a model soldier, one of his commanders called him into the office to tell him they could greatly advance his military career. He was keen to be promoted until he realised they wanted him to join the Freemasons to accomplish this process. Wisely he declined their offer and ended up leaving the armed forces.

Freemasonry of the Founding Fathers

Now the sad thing is that Freemasons have, over time, infiltrated the church and the American government. Many of our presidents were Freemasons, and still others were members of other, equally evil societies such as the Skull and Bones and Bohemian Grove.

The Founding Fathers who were Freemasons were committed to building a democracy that was based on a form of occultism called the Atlantean Scheme. The word "occult" means hidden. Contrast that idea with God, who doesn't hold secrets from us, but tells us everything He is doing.

John 15:15-17 *"Henceforth I call you not servants; for the servant knoweth not what his lord doeth: but I have called you friends; for all things that I have heard of my Father I have made known unto you. ¹⁶Ye have not chosen me, but I have chosen you, and ordained you, that ye should go and bring forth fruit, and that your fruit should remain: that whatsoever ye shall ask of the Father in my name, he may give it you. ¹⁷These things I command you, that ye love one another."*

Lucifer, an archangel whose name means "light" rebelled against God, and was given a new name: Satan. Now he will deceive the world and his ministers—such as the Freemasons and Illuminati—will commit terrible deeds.

2 Corinthians 11:13-15 *"For such are false apostles, deceitful workers, transforming themselves into the apostles of Christ. ¹⁴And no marvel; for Satan himself is transformed into an angel of light. (Lucifer the former archangel who chose the wrong career) ¹⁵Therefore it is no great thing if his ministers also be transformed as the ministers of righteousness; whose end shall be according to their works."*

Christians have been given the truth by the power of the Holy Spirit who dwells within us.

1 John 2:20 *"But ye have an unction from the Holy One, and ye know all things."*

Luke 8:10 *"And he said, Unto you it is given to know the mysteries of the kingdom of God: but to others in parables; that seeing they might not see, and hearing they might not understand."*

Note: any involvement where you were exposed in your life or in your generations to secret societies and lies such as "God is withholding good from you" (see Psalm 84:11), that is a possible open gateway where the devil has been given legal rights to bring the curses of Deut. 28 into your life. Go to God and repent for what you personally have done and renounce the things done by your ancestors, as was done in Nehemiah 9:2. God delights in releasing you from the manifestations of that evil and generously restores you in the name of Jesus.

The order of Freemasonry appears to only date back a few hundred years, however, in reality it probably began thousands of years ago. The lower degree Masons may ignorantly believe they are members of a social club, dedicated to helping each other and making the world a better place. But those at higher levels are fully aware and are hard at work to bring about evil. Consider this: the motto of highest level Thirty-Third Degree Masons is Or do Ab Chao, which means "order out of chaos". Although on the surface this seems benign, the New World Order they are seeking to establish necessitates the collapse of existing governments through organized chaos. After that, the people will be desperate for anything that promises peace, and that's when satanic "new leaders" can rise out of the ashes with their version of order and control.

Nimrod, of Genesis 10, was the first evil world ruler and built the tower of Babel. He is considered to be the very first Mason.

There were and still are numerous professing Christians, evangelists, and preachers who took the oaths/curses in the rituals of becoming Freemasons. God told us His people perish from lack of knowledge (Hosea 4:6). But that does not excuse our ignorance, which can be very costly.

Maybe this helps explain Matthew 7:22, *"Many will say to me in that day, Lord, Lord, have we not prophesied in thy name? and in thy name have cast out devils? and in thy name done many wonderful works?"*

The Atlantean Scheme the Freemasons devised, most likely with help from the kingdom of darkness, says that America was birthed out of Europe, and all of our presidents have come from the bloodlines of European royalty.

Francis Bacon, father of the "scientific method" and one of the most noteworthy Freemasons, was born in London on January 22, 1561. He served as Attorney General and Lord Chancellor of England until a parliamentary committee charged him with 23 separate counts of corruption. The king basically let him go after some political pressure, however due to his public disgrace, Bacon spent his time in pursuits of philosophical studies.

There are some indications that Bacon had gone into debt while secretly funding the publishing of materials for the Freemasons and Rosicrucians. He also published the "Spear Shakers," and "Knights of the Helmet," as well as plays and articles, with the assistance of a chap named Ben Jonson. Some believe he wrote a selection of the plays under the pen name "Shakespeare." Bacon's elevation to a place of great political influence would have certainly been hindered if it were known that he wrote plays for the commoners. Very possibly, writing as William Shakespeare was merely a front to shield his identity.

In the prime of his life, Bacon acquired the favour of numerous powerful and wealthy European. He and his cronies believed that there had been an original Atlantis the lost city of legend buried under the sea. They believe the Nephilim, the mighty men of renown from Greek Mythology, built and ruled it. At some point, the people of Atlantis disobeyed the Nephilim and the great city was destroyed and sank into the ocean.

Explorers have uncovered artifacts of giant sphinxes and pyramids located within the Bermuda Triangle off the shores of Cuba. It is believed this region was once dry land, but now only the island of Cuba still remains above water. Scientists Paul Weinzweig and Pauline Zalitzki went searching for evidence of Atlantis off the coast of Cuba. Using their robot submersible, they confirmed with photographic evidence that a gigantic city exists 600 feet below, at the bottom of the ocean.

Francis Bacon wrote a utopian novel called New Atlantis, which was published in 1627. It depicts a mythical island in the Pacific Ocean called Bensalem. Bacon's idea was to have the Freemasons build a new democracy based on this concept.

His unfinished novel inspired the formation of the Royal Society and played a leading role in creating the early American colonies. What's more, the Freemasons were receiving much of their funding for building this New Word Order in the New World. Numerous Europeans within the ranks of this cult were coming over to America for this purpose. At the time they could not budge the political power in Europe to go along with such sinister ideas so they found another place—America.

Now let me share an interesting quote by George Washington: "It is not my intention to doubt that the doctrine of the Illuminati and the principles of Jacobinism had not spread in the United States. On the contrary, no one is more satisfied of this fact than I am." He wrote this to the Reverend G. W. Snyder; the entire letter is published in the Writings of George Washington, p 518519.

The Jacobins were a radical, leftist group advocating egalitarian democracy and engaging in terrorist activities during the French Revolution of 1789. I recall Tom Horn's story of a politician who asked him if he was aware that concurrent at every presidential inauguration in Washington, D.C. an occult ritual is also held? Its purpose is to raise the spirit of Osiris from the underworld that it might enter into every U. S. president.

If that sounds far-fetched, you would be startled to learn about Bohemian Grove. This is a 2,700-acre campground in Monte Rio, California that belongs to a private men's club. In mid July, there is an annual two-week "retreat" where all manner of evil rituals are performed. In attendance are the world's power-elite, such as former U. S. presidents, Hollywood stars, and the ultra wealthy. Reporters and the mainstream media claim the group's activities are harmless. You be the judge of whether mock human sacrifices, the unleashing of demonic spirits into the crowd and prayers to Satan are just grown men having a little fun.

In Tom Horn's book Apollyon Rising 2012, he writes about the New World Order (novus ordo) being derived from the prophecies of the Cumaean Sibyl. She was a prophetess of Apollo for the Greeks, Osiris for the Egyptians, who predicted the return of this deity at a future date.

Revelation 9:11 *"And they had a king over them, which is the angel of the bottomless pit, whose name in the Hebrew tongue is Abaddon, but in the Greek tongue hath his name Apollyon."*

The Great Seal of the United States printed on the dollar bill contains Egyptian symbols, but the wording of the motto is suggestive of prophecies about Apollo, who we could also call the antichrist. According to the U. S. Bureau of Engraving and Printing, the seal reflects the beliefs and values that the Founding Fathers attached to the new nation and wished to pass on to their descendants. On the back side is the all-seeing eye of Horus. He was the son of Isis and Osiris, the god of the rising son, the bearer of light, Lucifer.

Could it be more than a mere coincidence that the American Seal also contains an Egyptian pyramid, an eagle, and sunburst? Some say these are symbols of the crossing of the Red Sea miracle and Israel's deliverance from the evil Pharaoh. Exodus 14 tells us how the Lord used a pillar of fire to hold back the Egyptian army until the Israelites were all able to cross over the Red Sea on dry ground. We read in Exodus 19:4, *"Ye have seen what I did unto the Egyptians, and how I bare you on eagles' wings, and brought you unto myself."*

So here we have eagle's wings taken as a sign of divine deliverance and protection. Does America's Coat of Arms simply represent divine protection, or is there more to this? You be the judge. Keep in mind, the man who oversaw the placing of those symbols on the dollar bill was President Franklyn Roosevelt, a 32-degree Mason who was keen on the "all-seeing eye." Freemasons revere a god they call "The Great Architect of the Universe." But this is not a name for God almighty.

I recall the time when an old friend, who became a Wall Street wizard, attended my first ever Christian concert in a church in upstate New Jersey. He came back stage and literally offered me a million dollars if I would stop right then and go back to playing secular rock and roll. He assured me he could buy my contract back from Atlantic Records and sign me with a new deal on Columbia Records. When I told him I can't do that, as my life now belongs to Jesus/Yeshua, he pulled out a hundred dollar bill with Benjamin Franklin's picture and said, "This is my god."

There are a number of prophesies you can find basically claiming Apollo will take his place to rule the universe one day. Some former members of the Illuminati have shared with me they were taught that at Armageddon the devil wins. He overthrows Jesus and locks up the Lord for a thousand years. The devil is the father of lies, taking Revelation 20:24 out of context.

Revelation 2:2-3 *And he laid hold on the dragon, that old serpent, which is the Devil, and Satan, and bound him a thousand years, And cast him into the bottomless pit, and shut him up, and set a seal upon him, that he should deceive the nations no more, till the thousand years should be fulfilled: and after that he must be loosed a little season.*

This is the crowd that supports people like Ted Turner who is in favor of saving the planet by eliminating some of the people. In an interview with Audubon Magazine, Turner said: "A total world population of 250300 million people, a 95 percent decline from present levels, would be ideal." I wonder if Mr. Turner shall lead by example? The elites are the same people who create the halftime performances of the Super Bowl and load them with their symbols and imagery.

Technology and Knowledge

The Apostle Paul says in 2 Thessalonians 2:3, *"Let no man deceive you by any means: for that day shall not come, except there come a falling away first, and that man of sin be revealed, the son of perdition;"*

Perdition is the Greek word "apolia," or Apollo, Apollyon.

Revelation 17:8 *"The beast that thou sawest was, and is not; and shall ascend out of the bottomless pit, and go into perdition: and they that dwell on the earth shall wonder, whose names were not written in the book of life from the foundation of the world, when they behold the beast that was, and is not, and yet is."*

Except for born-again believers, the world shall one day be deceived into wholesale idolatry. The remnant believers will suffer great persecution. We read in Romans 1:25 that they will change the truth of God into a lie, and worship and serve the creature more than the Creator. Again, when shall we, the Church, warn others? Before this happens, or after?

Skeptics and scoffers will argue that we are too smart for that. Just like the Bible said, knowledge has increased to the point where we are on information overload. Yet, consider this: Has wisdom increased as well as knowledge? One glance at social media will make this obvious! No, although we have more information than we will ever be able to comprehend, wisdom is crying in the streets for someone, anyone, to listen (see Prov. 1:20). The following examples of technological advances will give you some idea of how knowledge without godly wisdom can be dangerous.

The technologies are now in place where holographic images can be projected into the sky. These are not like old-time outdoor movies, but 3D images that look every bit real. Today, we would use a headset that looks like a giant pair of sunglasses that is a computer equipped with a holographic processing chip. Wearing the headset, you can see and interact with 3D images all around you, even pinching, pulling, and flicking them away. A homeowner could wear the headset to get help from a plumber miles away. Using his own computer, the plumber could "mark" the pipe to show the homeowner which one needs repair.

Holographic technology has been called "the transporting vehicle to move the internet from a 2D space to a 3D space." Some holographs are transparent, and other are not, which means you could walk around the image as if it were in the same room as you. This gives a new understanding of Revelation 13:15, *"And he had power to give life unto the image of the beast, that the image of the beast should both speak, and cause that as many as would not worship the image of the beast should be killed."* Likewise, it would be possible to mimic a false rapture or the sudden appearance of a messiah descending from the sky.

Could this be why the Lord Jesus/Yeshua forewarned us in places like Matthew 24:24, *"For there shall arise false Christs, and false prophets, and shall shew great signs and wonders; insomuch that, if it were possible, they shall deceive the very elect."*

Other technologies are being developed that will give one the ability to beam thoughts directly into people's heads. This kind of mind control could be used to condition us to accept the New World Order.

The World Economic Forum recently met in Davos, Switzerland to discuss, among other topics, the "Fourth Industrial Revolution." This describes a combination of technologies that blur the lines between the physical, digital, and biological. Examples are artificial intelligence (AI) like self-driving cars and drones, and the CRISPR gene-editing tool. James Clapper, U. S. Director of National Intelligence, added gene-editing to a list of threats posed by weapons of mass destruction and proliferation because of the potentially harmful biological agents that can be created. The basic ingredients for CRISPR can be purchased online for $60.

Scientists in the UK have been given governmental permission for one project to experiment on human embryos up to seven days old. The embryos, which are donated by IVF patients, are genetically altered, observed, then destroyed. This has huge implications and is taking mankind further into "free market eugenics" and to the creation of designer babies.

And while one branch of science is using biology to change mankind, another is transforming humanity through computer technology. This is the basic concept of trans humanism (H+), whose stated goal is to overcome mortality. They believe this is achievable by 2045—the same year, conservatively speaking, they believe man and machines will merge. Zoltan Istvan wrote a book called The Transhumanist Wager, and founded the Transhumanist Party. He and his followers believe that marriage won't make sense when humans live for a thousand years.

Zoltan Istvan said, "In the transhumanist age, it's time to leave behind closed-mindedness. In our relationships with others, we should instead look not with our biases and bigotry, but for what a person we care about can do for us, and what we can do for them. That person may be a human, a cyborg, a robot, or even a computer program. Whatever it is, frankly, is not important. It's what it does and how it does it. And if it does good, honest, and meaningful actions, then that's plenty upon which to build love, intimacy, and a successful future."

Let us remember that cell phones changed the world about 15 or 20 years ago. Almost everyone has one now, rich or poor, good or evil. Nomadic Mongolians who live in the Gobi desert now have cell phones and lap tops!

Zoltan Istvan also spoke about the evolution of pleasure. "And sex? Well, that can and will be better and more pleasurable with the rise of transhumanist technology. Already, scientists are working on pure outright stimulation of the erogenous zones in our brains. Stimulating this part of ourselves will be easier, on demand, and disease and pregnancy free. Of course, the coming world of virtual and augmented reality will also offer endless amounts of physical experimentation via haptic suits to satisfy one's lusts, too."

We are all watching the debates and insanity going on with the breakdown of morality and corruption surfacing with elected world leaders. We are watching the agenda unfolding of calling evil good and good evil now playing out (see Isaiah 5:20). We are also watching the threats of the breakdown of the family. The bottom line is that the Transhumanist movement is to replace man and women as God designed and intended with a new hybrid blended version. Just as in ancient Greek mythology where the hermaphrodite held a very respected position. When the male child of Hermes and Aphrodite fused his physical properties with a nymph, becoming a being composed of the physical traits of both sexes.

All those stories about the mighty gods and goddess's of ancient Greece seem to originate with the Nephilim accounts from Genesis 6:4. Keeping in mind today we have a new term of "Human Biotechnology," where science is developing artificial biogenetic parts like hearts and lungs and all manner of assorted body parts, working towards advancing the idea of Human .O2 of a race of immortal beings (see Genesis 3:4). Along with all the other bizarre accounts of demonic beings manifesting as disembodied invisible spirits such as a spirit of fear, unforgiveness or bitterness, trying to merge in your thought life as if they were your very own thoughts (see 2 Corinthians 10 :5). It seems these entities are appearing and masquerading as extraterrestrials or angels of light with increasing frequency (see 2 Corinthians 11:14-15). Culminating with the Great Deception that is going to happen according to verses like, 2 Thessalonians 2:10-11, *"And with all deceivableness of unrighteousness in them that perish; because they received not the love of the truth, that they might be saved. And for this cause God shall send them strong delusion, that they should believe a lie:"*

In the meantime we must carry on with the great commission and share the Gospel, heal the sick and cast out demons in the almighty name of Jesus/Yeshua. Stay in faith and keep your joy! The Lord Jesus/Yeshua is returning, so keep looking up!

Transhumanists really believe we will soon be immortal soon without having to ask the Lord Jesus/Yeshua to grant us eternal life. A friend in the UK called to tell me about undergoing a surgical procedure implant a microchip in order to reduce the pain, only it's not working so well, could I pray?

This is reminiscent of the fallen angels forcibly taking human women as their wives to corrupt our bloodlines. Thus the Lord made a way for Noah and his family to escape, keeping their line from contamination.

One thing is certain, the deception will be so clever and powerful as to become nearly inescapable, according to Matthew 24:22, *"And except those days should be shortened, there should no flesh be saved: but for the elect's sake those days shall be shortened."*

Maybe at some point they'll take some DNA from a Nephilim sample and mix it with human DNA to create the Antichrist. Scientists are already mixing human and animal genes in laboratories around the world. The Bible tells us of numerous strange creatures in the Old Testament. Some were half-human and half-animal as told in Isaiah 13:21, *"But wild beasts of the desert shall lie there; and their houses shall be full of doleful creatures; and owls shall dwell there, and satyrs shall dance there."* Many of us were taught that satyrs—horned creatures with the upper bodies of men and the lower parts of goats—were just myths. I'm not so sure, especially since today we have the technology to mix species.

When most people hear about stem cell research, they don't seem to connect the fact that this is the kingdom of Satan trying to improve upon God's creation. I believe this also happened in the days of Noah. My saying this will make some people nervous. It seems that today, just doing a modest amount of research on these things will have the world label you a conspiracy theorist. My personal definition of a conspiracy theorist is someone whose research is often being disproved and dismissed to fit the paradigm of political correctness.

DARPA

I am aware how astonishing and unbelievable many of the things I am sharing must seem. We are indeed in unprecedented times; however, it's best to understand what is unfolding on the world stage with a view to how it is fulfilling Bible prophesies.

There are some upper-echelon government advisers having some dreams and visions coming right out of science fiction. They all appear to be communicating from a oneworld agenda. Let us consider how DARPA (Defense Advanced Research Projects Agencies) has an approved budget of tens of millions of dollars in an effort to create a new genetic blueprint for humanity.

DARPA is an agency of the U. S. Department of Defense responsible for the development of emerging technologies for use by the military. DARPA was created in 1958 as the Advanced Research Projects Agency by President Dwight D. Eisenhower, and is now one of the largest federal agencies. It is tasked with innovation—often in conjunction with private laboratories—to such things as rewriting the DNA of American soldiers. This is a federally sanctioned use of tax dollars to produce transhuman super-soldiers.

As the transhumanists see it, this new type of soldier will be part animal and part human— think eyes of a tiger, strength and endurance of an elephant, and body of a human athlete.

The Pentagon is also developing a high bandwidth neural interface that would allow people to transfer and loop data from their minds to external devices, perhaps being able to control a drone or computer with by thought. In essence, people become computerized beings.

DARPA has already announced the first successful tests on animals using tiny sensors that travel through blood vessels, lodge in the brain, and record neural activity using a stentrode, which combines a stent and electrode smaller than the size of a paperclip.

The injectable machine was developed by neurologist Tom Oxley and his team from the University of Melbourne in Australia. They came up with a way to insert a transmitter into the brain without actually having to drill a hole. Doug Weber, a member and program manager of DARPA has said, "By reducing the need for invasive surgery, the stentrode may pave the way for more practical implementations of those kinds of life-changing applications of brain machine interfaces.

There is an independent group of scientists called the JA-SONs who has been assembled to advise the United States government on matters of science and technology. They are mostly working to advance our military powers by using health informatics, cyber-warfare and renewable energy—at least that's the unclassified research. The classified projects involve changing weather patterns and using acid rain to ensure we can dominate on any battlefield.

The Mark of the Beast

There are researchers today that suggest this could be one way the mark of the beast might be used to alter humans so that they're no longer redeemable. They can literally use some device going through their bodily systems and rewrite their genetic makeup using a Vector.

Vector (biology) traditionally used in medicine, is an organism that does not cause disease itself but which spreads infection by conveying pathogens from one host to another. Species of mosquito, for example, serve as vectors for the deadly disease Malaria.

The National Institutes of Health—another government-funded U. S. government organisation—uses tax dollars for health-related advanced science and research. They also give large grants to universities that are developing documents that will outline the constitutional rights of non-humans—or humans of the future—whose genetic makeup have been significantly altered. In 2006, President George W. Bush in his State of the Union Address urged legislators to take the necessary steps to stop the rise of human-animal hybrids. Ohio and Arizona have already put the laws on their books.

Have you ever heard of a talking horse? Well, one day Mr. Ed (TV's talking horse) might be teaching at the university level. What about that donkey who spoke in Numbers 22? He made more sense than the prophet he was talking to. Just image how the world might change when half human/animals/whatever are granted the right to vote!

Mind you, they shall validate these ideas by connecting them to the eradication of disease. Biotechnology is at the stage now where scientists can extract liver cells from a person, insert them into a developing sheep, and then harvest a human liver made from a person's own cells. For someone with liver disease, this is good news!

The Brookings Institution, which is an American think-tank in Washington, D. C., conducts research for education in the social sciences. One of their projects is a new series called The Future of the Constitution in which they cover such as things as cyber security and unreasonable search and seizures in the information age. However they are also saying that within 10 years we will be creating genetically engineered, alternative gender beings who will need a Bill of Rights and constitutional privileges.

Some in the Church have recognized the need to wake up. Consider this quote by David Bay, Cutting Edge Ministries:

"America was designated as the New Atlantis that would lead the world to the Antichrist. The original national bird envisioned by our Masonic leadership in the late 1700s was not the American Eagle, but the Phoenix Bird. This historic fact strongly suggests that, at the right moment in world history, with the world entering through the portals of the Kingdom of Antichrist, America might suddenly be immolated in fiery flames, burning to the ashes; out of these ashes, the New World Order would arise."

This begs the question of how these organisations can establish their utopian world with so many Bible believing people still on earth. Those of us who understand ancient prophesy may actually be hindering the New World Order.

Demons and Shape-Shifters

We have taught that from the Scriptures that demons are invisible disembodied spirits that need permission to access your body so they can express themselves and their nature through you. Where did they come from? Could they be the spirits of the giants/Nephilim whose bodies drowned in the flood? The world was probably overrun with them at that time, so they would have numbered in the millions or billions. They were called the 'Mighty Men of Renown' and were probably created by the fallen angels. These are called Gibborim/giants in the original Hebrew, and also called the "watchers" in Genesis 6:4. Clearly they were the half breeds, angelic hybrids, or titans—titanos in Greek, which means "greys."

Is it possible that the fallen angels changed shapes, or shape-shifted into a form of human beings so they could have intercourse with women? Did they purposely do this, understanding they would cause some aberrant genetic changes to occur? Their offspring, the giants, seem to be proof of this aberration.

We read in Deuteronomy 3:11 *"For only Og king of Bashan remained of the remnant of giants; behold, his bedstead was a bedstead of iron; is it not in Rabbath of the children of Ammon? nine cubits was the length thereof, and four cubits the breadth of it, after the cubit of a man."*

The King of Bashan had a bed that was 13 to 15 feet long; and Goliath was six cubits tall (9 or 10 feet). Other aberrations were they had 12 fingers, 12 toes and double rows of teeth. There appears to be no records of these perversities prior to the intervention of the watchers. These dormant genetic tendencies still surface today in people round the world. The watchers may have been created by God as some sort of guardians assigned to watch over the earth and protect mankind from just this sort of thing happening. But like Satan, they too failed miserably in their assignment.

What sort of battles were being fought in the heavens that it took 21 days for the Lord's angels to reach Daniel?

Daniel 10:13 *"But the prince of the kingdom of Persia withstood me one and twenty days: but, lo, Michael, one of the chief princes, came to help me; and I remained there with the kings of Persia."*

Have you heard about the Book of Enoch? It and other such books were once part of the King James Bible. Many insights and plans for the future are in the Book of Enoch and have made quite an impact in academic circles. It is properly known as First Enoch and has been authenticated as existing before the Church Age. A number of scholars date it 200 BC. There were multiple copies discovered in 1948 as part of the Dead Sea Scrolls.

Other ancient books like Jubilees, The Book of Jasher, and Testimony of the Twelve Patriarchs, mirror the biblical account of fallen angels (or "watchers," as they are called in those books) who rebelled against God and attempted to enslave the whole world.

Joshua 10:13 and 2 Samuel 1:18 both refer to The Book of Jasher. It covers much of the same ground as the Bible from creation to the death of Moses. According to Jasher, the Watchers experimented with the DNA of mankind and animals, thus creating Nephilim. Mind you, this book was written thousands of years ago! They may have also produced such creatures as the Pegasus, minotaur, unicorn, and dinosaurs. There are indications that the Watchers wanted a source of food for their offspring. Maybe they were simply making a dino-burger?

We read in Jude 6 the acts of these fallen angels brought about tremendous consequences for them: Jude 1:6, "And the angels which kept not their first estate, but left their own habitation, he hath reserved in everlasting chains under darkness unto the judgment of the great day."

UFOs and Alien Beings

UFOs are being seen all over the world. Reports show there are more than 2,000 sightings a month, and I believe this is part of the great deception. It is obvious that some form of intelligent alien entities have been interacting with humans. Angels and demons are beings from another atmosphere—space or another heavenly dimension—that also interact with us. Demons certainly communicate with us spirit-to-spirit. Did you ever have an evil thought and wonder, Now where did that come from?

Any communication from these supposed alien travelers are contrary to the teachings of Christianity. Their basic message, supported by Hollywood, is that human beings are close to evolving into a higher advanced state. Their role is to help us reach it.

It seems to me these beings are really the fallen angels who serve the devil, and their real agenda is to establish Satan's kingdom—possibly through genetically altering the human species. The Lord Jesus cannot come for them as Kinsman Redeemer, like He will for us.

The Lord gave us things like science, quantum physics and the gift of critical thinking. We look at the Word of God and the ministry of the Lord Jesus/Yeshua while He was on this earth and we are God-smacked! No other religious leader is able to even come close to what He accomplished. Yet, the world has been taught to take a negative view of supernatural facts from the Bible because those things do not submit to the theory of evolution. Without evolution, there is no path forward for socialism, which makes way for communism. Many world leaders and those at the helm of organisations such as the U. S. Department of Health, Education, and Welfare and the United Nations are devoted evolutionists. Do you suppose their appointments are accidental? Or are these things happening because of an invisible demonic power manipulating men and events?

All who report to Satan know that if they continue to tell the same lies, eventually people shall accept lies as truth. Adolf Hitler once said, "Make the lie big, make it simple, keep saying it, and eventually they will believe it." Lenin was quoted as saying, "A lie told often enough becomes the truth."

These strategies did not die with those men because it is not only about the humans who were used, it is even more about the invisible kingdom of Ephesians 6:12: *"For we wrestle not against flesh and blood, but against principalities, against powers, against the rulers of the darkness of this world, against spiritual wickedness in high places."* We are to put on the whole armour of God so that we may be able to stand against the wiles of the devil.

There is a direct link between the agenda of the enemy through spirits of darkness and the evil committed by radical Islam. Consider Cain who murdered his brother, Abel. The spirits of envy and jealousy made way for the spirit of murder.

Genesis 4:10-11 *"And he said, What hast thou done? the voice of thy brother's blood crieth unto me from the ground. And now art thou cursed from the earth, which hath opened her mouth to receive thy brother's blood from thy hand;"*

Today that blood can still be heard crying from the earth. The blood of men, women and children from every race and every part of the world will continue to cry out until the Lord comes to right every wrong.

Cain reaped the curse of his actions and was exiled by the Lord.

Genesis 4:12 *"When thou tillest the ground, it shall not henceforth yield unto thee her strength; a fugitive and a vagabond shalt thou be in the earth."*

Chapter Seven

THE NAZIS AND THE INFORMATION AGE

The Nazis were experts at brainwashing. They used propaganda so effectively, one could imagine they were demonically influenced. From movies and music, to art, radio, and the printed word, the Nazis manipulated perceptions and caused the German people to put away their ability to think critically. How else could an entire nation be conned? They obviously tapped into some very demonically inspired information.

Don't be surprised when one day the antichrist uses Twitter, Instagram, Pinterest and Facebook to manipulate the masses!

Consider this also, Hitler's book was called Mein Kampf. It was the "final solution" of how to get rid of the Jews. Today that is repackaged in the spirit of Jihad, which is translated, "my struggle, my holy war—or *Mein Kampf* in German.

Before the flood of Noah, there may have been some extraordinary advances in technologies we still have not uncovered. It seems they may have had global communication similar to what we have today. There are evidences that suggest technology could have been engineered in the monstrous stone blocks found in Peru and other places throughout the world.

The Nazi intellectuals had accessed the occult to such a place where they received ideas for advanced technologies. For example, their Vril Society and Thule's Society worked behind the scenes to bring Hitler to power. Both groups had practicing clairvoyants. During séances, they received occultic blueprints and rather highly sophisticated diagrams on how to build an-tigravity machines, atomic bombs, and other tools of destruc-tion. Those Nazi scientists were probably many more years ad-vanced at the time than the Allied side.

They were into genetics, rocketry, mind control, electro-magnetic fields (EMF), and scalar technology, which led to products designed to protect the human nervous system from the hazards of man-made electromagnetic fields (EMF). After World War II, it was Nazi scientists like Werner Von Braun who helped start NASA! Some of the worst tragedies committed by the Nazis happened as they experimented with DNA and cre-ated deformed humans. The pictures are some of the most disturbing I have ever seen.

The Nazis also held theories about the Nephilim. They be-lieved that before the flood, the Nephilim lived in a place called Hyper-borea, a far-northern land that was also the secret place of origin for the Aryan race. The Nazis believed they were descended from the Nephilim—a superiour race of Nordics.

Hitler's rise to power is instructive in that it was incredibly similar in many ways to what we are experiencing today, es-pecially related to the manipulation of monetary supplies and systems. The whole world is now set up to experience hyperin-flation as part of that demonic long-term plan for the NWO to destroy the dollar and America as a superpower.

Don't miss the NWO's work through entertainment and in-formation to use psychological programming and mind con-trol. This is not a new concept. There is nothing new under the sun (Ecc. 1:9). Carl Jung admitted that everything he learned about psychology was taught to him by Philemon, his spirit guide, another name for demon. Jung's research asserts the concept of an impersonal or "collective unconscious"—a sort of library which contains everything one has ever known. Where would he get an idea like that from? Jung was deeply involved in the occult. Along with his mother and two female cousins, he conducted hypnotically induced séances which opened the door to the demonic realm. Scripture says it is an abomination to engage in such practices. Besides Philemon, Jung also chan-neled other spirits. Could we say the man was possessed?

Dr. Jung wrote about his spirit guides in his book Memo-ries, Dreams, Reflections: "Philemon and other figures of my fantasies brought home to me the crucial insight that there are things in the psyche which I do not produce, but which produce themselves and have their own life. Philemon represented a force that was not myself. In my fantasies, I held conversations with him, and he said things which I had not consciously thought. Psychologically, Philemon represented superior insight."

Jung's father, Paul Achilles Jung, was a pastor. His preaching was along the style of some churches today—devoid of any true power of God. He was also intrigued by Catholic mysticism and conducted seminars on the teachings of Ignatius Loyola, who founded the Jesuit order. His son Carl was probably not taught to test the spirits! If so, he would have found Satan masquerading as an angel of light. The apostle John warned: *"Do not believe every spirit, but test the spirits to see whether they are from God because many false prophets have gone out into the world"* (1 John 4:1).

In his original writings, Jung called these beings "archetypes and evil spirits," later changing it to "dark shadows and archetypes." Perhaps he wanted to be more politically correct. He also taught people to channel Anima, the female soul, and Animus the male soul. The Lord made man and woman, not combinations. Now we have the indoctrination of this belief through the trans-gender movement, another false doctrine so successfully introduced that people don't see the evil for what it is. Many are even viewing God as both male and female.

Now that we have connected the dots, do you see that the New World Order (NWO), did not begin with the Nazis—nor start with Francis Bacon's secret plan for the new Atlantis—aka the United States of America? It wasn't even birthed with the Nephilim! No, the beginning came with Lucifer who exalted himself above God. And in his rebellion he took one-third of all the angels with him, who then infected humanity with their seed through the Nephilim. They have been influencing men's thoughts and actions throughout history.

Fortunately, the Lord has placed watchmen on the wall for such a time as this.

Ezekiel 33:6 *"But if the watchman see the sword come, and blow not the trumpet, and the people be not warned; if the sword come, and take [any] person from among them, he is tak-*

en away in his iniquity; but his blood will I require at the watchman's hand."

Does see yourself in these end times as a watchman? You are observing the enemy gathering outside the church walls. Are you beginning to understand what is happening and what is coming?

Matthew 24:6-8 *"And ye shall hear of wars and rumours of wars: see that ye be not troubled: for all these things must come to pass, but the end is not yet. ⁷For nation shall rise against nation, and kingdom against kingdom: and there shall be famines, and pestilences, and earthquakes, in divers places. ⁸All these are the beginning of sorrows."*

We are certainly seeing some sorrows now, yet the worst is still to come. All the power of hell will be unleashed, and even the powers of heaven will be shaken.

Luke 21:26 *"Men's hearts failing them for fear, and for looking after those things which are coming on the earth: for the powers of heaven shall be shaken."*

Many of us feel desperate to warn others that they must make their peace with God. At times I get a wee bit frustrated that they are not very interested! Even Christians ask me why I am "so negative." They must be under the delusion that things are going to carry on as they have been, our trillion-dollar debt, social disintegration, national unrest, and on it goes. Only some of the Christians connect a removal of God from our culture and sin run amok as a reason for our troubles. A recent Barna poll showed 90 percent of America's pastors do not preach about repentance and reading the Scriptures. The mind-set of the Church is just look at the good in everything, and it will all work out. But scriptures clearly tell us to discern both good and evil, for that describes a mature believer.

Hebrews 5:14 *"But strong meat belongeth to them that are of full age, even those who by reason of use have their senses exercised to discern both good and evil."*

Some will continue to ignore the warnings, and others will react in fear. Neither is a correct response. Instead, we need to keep praying and keep looking up and comforting each other with God's promises. One day, the Lord himself shall descend from heaven with a shout, and with the voice of the archangel the sound of the trump of God. The dead in Christ shall rise first, then we which are alive and remain shall be caught up together with them in the clouds. We will meet the Lord in the air—and so we shall ever be with the Lord! (1 Thess. 4:17, 18)

Perhaps you have noticed that many of the sheep are not listening. The watchmen are blowing the trumpets and shouting the alarm, but only a few people take a real interest.

The Dis-Information Age

So, my question then becomes, Why do you suppose it is so difficult to wake people up?

Think back to the beginning of this book. Why did my pastor friend from back in chapter one and his cohorts try so hard to dismiss these subjects? Is there a concerted effort to destroy mankind's ability to think? I believe you now know the answer to these questions. And if you are still skeptical, I understand. That's why I am asking you to take everything here before the Lord. Ask Him what He thinks.

Now, let's also consider the information age and the enemy's desire to corrupt it.

Have you ever noticed that news reporters on mainstream television all saying the same things? For example, local reporters from all over America are all saying, verbatim, "You don't need us to tell you that the price of oil is back on the rise." It appears all the major news outlets simply repeat the same lines and phrases. This suggests they are either lazy and copying each other, or that one source is dictating their scripts. It has gotten so bad that comedians such as John Stewart are poking fun at them!

Sometimes the powers behind the scenes tell us the planet is running out of oil to justify raising prices. Then during an election year, strangely, the prices come way down. Oil is like the lifeblood of the modern world and wars have been fought to secure access to it. Could we be on our way to another D-Day type of invasion over oil? We cannot overestimate the times that the hand of our Lord has held back the tide of war and saved us from destruction.

We are surrounded by those who desire to change the world and trade the gospel truth for a deceptive lie. Can biblical truth coexist with things like atheism? Former President George Bush and others of like mind have repeatedly made such statements that all religions, whether they be Muslim, Christian, or any other, all pray to the same God.

Can Allah and the God of the Holy Bible be one and the same? A modest amount of research reveals Allah is also known as the Arabian Moon god, who is also known in ancient times as Baal, Hubal, and Molech. Hubal was worshipped at the Kaaba in Mecca in pre-Islam days. During Muhammed's lifetime, children were sacrificed into the fire of the idol Molech.

Leviticus 18:21 *"And thou shalt not let any of thy seed pass through the fire to Molech, neither shalt thou profane the name of thy God: I am the LORD."*

Molech was also known as a Canaan and a Phoenician deity. Statues of Molech were made of brass having the face of an ox, and the body of a man with arms outstretched. Infants were placed in the statue's hands and burnt with fire. Accounts tell of the priests beating drums during these times of ritual sacrifice, perhaps as a way to help drown out the baby's screams so as to hinder anyone who might have any compassion and attempt to rescue the child.

2 Kings 23:10 *"And he defiled Topheth, which is in the valley of the children of Hinnom, that no man might make his son or his daughter to pass through the fire to Molech."*

This same misunderstanding of who God is and what He does can be found in the Illuminati and the New World Order. These elites believe that Satan is mankind's helper, whilst God is mankind's enemy. They dispute the entire creation account and reinterpret Genesis 3 to suggest that the serpent was trying to bring about a cosmic awakening. Genesis 3:45 And the serpent said unto the woman, Ye shall not surely die: 4For God doth know that in the day ye eat thereof, then your eyes shall be opened, and ye shall be as gods, knowing good and evil.

After all, they believe Lucifer/Satan is a light-bringer.

This group of elites includes the richest and most powerful people in the world. Some of the other associations that line up with this mind-set of controlling the world and ushering in a new order include the Bilderbergs, the Council on Foreign Relations, and the Trilateral Commission. In his memoirs, renowned billionaire David Rockefeller, who is part of this elite group, wrote, "...We are part of a secret cabal working against the best interest of the United States... If that's the charge, I stand guilty, and I am proud of it." For more on these agencies and their agendas, consult the internet and you will find a wealth of information.

UFOs have intrigued people of all cultures and the majority of those writing about them believe their appearance is a good thing happening to this fallen world! For example, the Vatican's astrophysicists and astrobiologists see this as part of the coming enlightenment. In order for their agenda to come into effect, the Holy Bible has to be discredited and people's faith in God must be destroyed. This can never be done with honesty, even though the unsaved person often thinks they are basically good, and if there is an afterlife they will somehow go to heaven.

One of my celebrity friends was once fascinated with UFOs at the height of his worldly popularity. One day, whilst in his hotel room, he was listening to an evangelist share the gospel and realised he was hearing the absolute truth. He made a life-changing decision and accepted Jesus Christ of Nazareth as His Saviour through tears of repentance. Soon afterwards he picked up a Bible that the Gideons had placed in his hotel room and began to read. The first thing he read was the account in Ezekiel where the prophet describes what appears to be a flying chariot, having wheels within wheels, and powered by angelic beings.

My friend realised the Lord was meeting him right where he was at that moment and giving him profound understanding that all the answers to about life and the universe are to be found within the Bible.

2 Timothy 3:16-17 *"All scripture is given by inspiration of God, and is profitable for doctrine, for reproof, for correction, for instruction in righteousness: 17That the man of God may be perfect, thoroughly furnished unto all good works."*

The Bible as we know it came into existence during the Council of Nicaea in 325 AD and the Council of Constantinople in 381 AD. That's when it was determined which ancient writings were to be included, and which were to be left out. Throughout the centuries, every doctrine has come under scholarly examination. It is debated first within groups of intellectuals who reach certain conclusions. Those then filter down into societies as the final word on the subject. Even though the debate ut whether Christ's return would be before or after the millium goes on today, the issue was actually settled long ago. In the 1900s, the second advent of Christ was put under the best microscope available at the time and conclusions were formed in favor of the pre-millennial return of Jesus Christ of Nazareth. It was believed there will be two separate events: first, the Church will be caught up with Christ together forever in the air; and next, Christ will return to put the world back into proper order during His 1,000year reign. Afterwards, the Lord will release the devil who will be wage one final war before being defeated by Christ. Then he shall be cast into the lake of fire forever.

Revelation 20:7-10, *"And when the thousand years are expired, Satan shall be loosed out of his prison, ⁸and shall go out to deceive the nations which are in the four quarters of the earth, Gog and Magog, to gather them together to battle: the number of whom is as the sand of the sea. ⁹And they went up on the breadth of the earth, and compassed the camp of the saints about, and the beloved city: and fire came down from God out of heaven and devoured them. ¹⁰And the devil that deceived them was cast into the lake of fire and brimstone, where the beast and the false prophet are, and shall be tormented day and night forever and ever."*

The Nephilim shall once again appear on this earth before the return of Christ. As we look into the ancient writings and into the Scriptures, we see there are several categories describing these beings, and several descriptions given by eyewitnesses who have seen them in modern times. Many tell of have encountered the Grays—the slim slant-eyed creatures we are familiar with from movies, television and books—who I believe may be an embodiment of dead Nephilim.

We also have archeological evidence of the Nordics—the beings associated with Nazi Aryanism. Thousands of Viking artifacts have been discovered that are thought to depict the Hammer of Thor. Thor, the god of thunder, allegedly used his hammer to protect Asgard, the celestial city of the gods. Thousands of crosses used for protection against the Nephilim have also been discovered. To me, this is more than mere mythology; it is confirmation of Genesis 6:4 and of such extra-biblical narratives as we have in the book of Enoch. Why would you need such protection unless the Nephilim were evil?

Hollywood's Contributions

Today we also hear accounts of the mysterious "men in black" who are more than just the heroes of a hit movie. They seem to appear along with sightings and encounters with UFOs. These aliens intimidate people to such an extent that they will not talk about the experience.

Now, keep in mind that these are demonic beings, and not friendly ETs from a distant planet. The Bible plainly speaks of evil spirits just as it does of the fallen angels and their half-human offspring. Is it out of the question to take a step further and suggest this may be occurring even now? Could we soon see the ungodly products of a breeding program put in place to infest the human race with demonic DNA—just as was done in Genesis 6?

Have you noticed that most everything I have discussed so far has been the subject of Hollywood movies and television shows?

Back in 1960s, there was a science-fiction comedy show called My Favourite Martian. The television series featured a human-looking extraterrestrial who crashed in a one-man spaceship near Los Angeles. This friendly anthropologist from Mars who finds himself stranded on planet Earth is befriended by a young newspaper reporter. The man takes him in as a roommate and introduces him as his "Uncle Martin."

Mind you, Uncle Martin refuses to reveal himself to anyone else other than his new roommate to avoid publicity or world-wide panic. He can raise two retractable antennae from his head and become invisible at will. If that is not enough, he has amazing telepathic abilities and can read and influence other people's minds. In fact, he can levitate objects simply using the motion of his finger. He was able to freeze people or speed them up. Unlike other shows that featured witches and genies, such as Bewitched and I Dream of Jeannie, or talking horses like Mr. Ed, or people transformed into objects, like My Mother the Car, My Favourite Martian was making way for the concept of superiour alien life-forms.

Episodes of The X-Files have women being abducted and impregnated by ETs, then the offspring are removed from the womb before birth—all with the government's consent! It used to seem like science fiction to me, but not so much any more!

What better way to introduce these ideas to the general public? We become so accustomed to these weird ideas that we are now numb. Will we one day become so brainwashed that we will believe what ETs tell us over what the Word of God is saying?

You see, by the time ET, Star Trek, Star Wars, Battle Star Galactica, X-Files, and others arrived, Hollywood had conditioned us to believe that we are not alone in the universe. We are primed to accept what would have once been deemed unimaginable.

When it comes to UFOs, remember that angels—those fallen and those obediently serving God—do not need flying machines. They travel in the same manner as the Lord did after His resurrection.

Acts 1:11 *"Which also said, Ye men of Galilee, why stand ye gazing up into heaven? this same Jesus, which is taken up from you into heaven, shall so come in like manner as ye have seen him go into heaven."*

There were many accounts in the Bible where people appeared and disappeared. They didn't need a flying machine.

To reiterate from chapter three, the Honorable Paul Hellyer—Canada's former Minister of Defense who had access to all sorts of top secret information—said these aliens are your friends, able to travel in spaceships and enter Earth through portals hidden in places like the Andes Mountains. He contends they have been visiting the Earth for thousands of years and continue to supply us with advanced technology. In fact, recent tallies show there are around 2,000 reports of UFO sightings and alien interactions per month worldwide! Now, I can agree with Hellyer that our advanced technology may have come from somewhere else. I just happen to believe the Bible, which credits Satan for tempting mankind with the knowledge of evil.

Is it possible that Satan's emmissaries, the demons, will be introduced to us as "helpers from another planet" who have come to help us in exchange for our allegiance? Perhaps they will offer even more advanced knowledge, especially in the fields of medicine, biotechnology and GMO crop production in exchange for our dominion over our physical bodies.

According to Hellyer, these superiour intelligent aliens are also well organised into what they call the "federation." They all adhere to "directive" which states that they can't involve themselves in the affairs of mankind unless they're invited to do so. Again this is reminiscent of all demons who need permission to come and torment you.

1 Timothy 4:13 *"Now the Spirit speaketh expressly, that in the latter times some shall depart from the faith, giving heed to seducing spirits, and doctrines of devils; 2speaking lies in hypocrisy; having their conscience seared with a hot iron; 3forbidding to marry, and commanding to abstain from meats, which God hath created to be received with thanksgiving of them which believe and know the truth."*

I have never been a fan of such shows as Star Trek, but it seems to me they are all propaganda designed to condition us to accept other life forms as our brothers and sisters. How exciting shall it be when the Vatican gets to water-baptise one of our extraterrestrial "friends"!

If we are not prepared to understand what is happening according to the Word of God, I dare say we shall be in a good deal of trouble on many levels. It seems likely most of the world is going to accept this idea that beings from some other galaxy started life on Earth and began all the religions of the world. Maybe these superior beings will arrive just in time at this critical juncture in history to save us from ourselves. Perhaps they will offer a microchip that will prevent you from ever becoming sick with disease, causing one to live hundreds of years as in the days of Noah. Many people will likely take this bait along with the plans that are presented for prosperity. Even worse, many of God's people will perish from lack of knowledge.

So what does this have to do with the return of Christ? Why is this so important to you? How is this helping you in your day-to-day issues? Where in the Bible is all this UFO phenomena written? The Bible tells us there is a first and third Heaven. We know from the Book of Job that the devil is able to walk up and down in the Earth.

Job 1:7 *"And the LORD said unto Satan, Whence comest thou? Then Satan answered the LORD, and said, From going to and fro in the earth, and from walking up and down in it."*

At some point, the devil and his demons will lose the ability to go between dimensions. Until then, we are in a war with these invisible beings.

I have been watching this thing unfold since I was first saved in the 70s and I did some illustrations for a UFO magazine. I was shown some extraordinary footage of strange crafts appearing and disappearing on eight millimeter film. This was before the invention of photoshop and other such advances in film manipulation. I have studied this a long time and met many people who had an encounter with the pilots of these crafts. Not one who had a close encounter with the evil spirit of Occultism behind this phenomena ever came away the better for it.

Some have described being abducted as a toddler and having strange beings probing their private parts. There are countless reports of these sorts of things going on with young children. I believe the devil knows he is outnumbered and is working diligently to destroy DNA and altering the gene pool like he tried before the flood of Noah's day. One account tells of a teacher whose student was able to read the headlines of a newspaper through the souls of their feet, blindfolded. Unnatural abilities could be indicative of trans humanism or demonic interference.

The good news is anything the devil tries, God will always outmaneuver him. Just as he did at the cross of Jesus and His glorious resurrection.

My friends Dr. L. A. Marzulli and Richard Shaw have dealt with many strange cases. They have shared about a man who was five years old when evil spirits masquerading as ETs came and took him on a journey. Marzulli and Shaw call him a "frequent flyer," meaning a person who is abducted many times. Now, after decades of encounters, he is finally coming forward to receive ministry. During one of the encounters with these evil spirits, a device was implanted in the man's leg. This story is told in Watchers 7: UFOs the Physical Evidence, and Watchers 8.

Marzulli and Shaw took the man to Dr. Roger Leir, who agreed to remove the implant. It showed up quite clearly on X-ray, ultra sound, and CAT scan, however, when it was time to remove the implant, it suddenly disappeared! It was as if some unseen forces wanted to hide it from the surgeons—who were not Christians. After watching the doctors trying to relocate the implant for about 45 minutes Marzulli suddenly felt the instruction of the Holy Spirit to pray. With the courage of his faith and conviction, Marzulli stepped forward saying to the room full of doctors, scientists and researchers, "Yes I know this may sound strange to you but I must pray right now to my God." He added something like, "If something unseen is hiding this implant from us, in the name of Jesus/Yeshua, may it be revealed now." Within a minute the implant came forward on the monitors, and in a supernatural way, submitted itself to the name of Jesus.

Marzulli and Shaw have assured me that moment was not lost on any of those who were in the operating theater!

I recall Marzulli and Shaw telling me about the late Dr. Roger Leir operating on patients who wanted the implants taken out. Dr. Leir initially was reluctant to deal with such cases and thought the patients needed a psychiatrist not a surgeon. However, after Dr. Leir was finally convinced of seeing the odd looking objects on the patients X-Ray's he decided to operate. To his absolute astonishment, what he discovered was a very tiny metallic implant and over the implant was a strange looking membrane of some sort of unknown secretion. Dr. Leir applies his scalpel and discovers that as he tries to cut this membrane, he can't penetrate it. He then takes forceps and yanks the metallic looking implant out. (See pictures)

The implant ended up breaking into two or three pieces. He places them in a Petri dish and still covered with some of the patient's own blood. He leaves them alone for some hours. They were separated by perhaps by a half an inch or an inch. The next day Dr. Leir discovers the pieces have tried to reassemble themselves back together, which is as strange to contemplate as the objects themselves.

Researching the implants, he has taken out of numerous patients, it was discovered they are giving out a clock speed of a frequency, which Dr. Leir and his associates think is possibly a saw tooth wave, which essentially means it's some sort of similar frequency to what we have in computer waves. It has a clock speed at 300 gigahertz, which is at least a hundred times faster than the fastest computer we know about today on earth. Upon closer examination Dr. Leir found inside these implants are carbon nano tubes which are not found in nature and the metal properties are like nothing we have on earth. The closest similarities would be that of the metal properties found in meteorites. This begs the question, "What are these implants for?" Dr. Leir thinks they are obviously changing a persons DNA. I know from my research that I collected for writing my book, What Was I Thinking? our thoughts are actually able to change our DNA which is why Our Holy Guide Book to the Supernatural tells us to take every thought captive to Christ. Are these implants a prototype of the Mark of the Beast? Are we living in the times the Lord Jesus/Yeshua forewarned us about before His return that it will be as in the Days of Noah?

Dr. Leir performed 17 of these operations before he passed away unexpectedly the 4th of January 2014.

Chapter Eight

ISRAEL AND THE MIDDLE EAST IN PROPHECY

I don't want you to be caught off guard! Now is the time to get right with the Lord. Now is the time to forgive everyone, including yourself, and accept the amazing mercy, grace and love of the Lord Jesus. The constant threat of Islamic terrorism, including the Moslem Brotherhood in Egypt, Hezbollah and HAMAS, ISIS and Iran imperil the whole world. They have also made it crystal clear what their intentions are for Israel. Remember that there is an invisible force behind the scenes that simply hates God's chosen people. Sometimes it seems it would be easier to unravel a plate of cooked spaghetti and place it back in the box than to straighten out this world. However, the Bible tells us not to be troubled and not to fear what we see today or in the future.

Mark 13:7 *"And when ye shall hear of wars and rumours of wars, be ye not troubled: for such things must needs be; but the end shall not be yet."*

There is no need for me to do a recap of the news and site all the Biblical indicators pointing to World War III starting in the Middle East anytime now. We know it's coming, we just don't know when precisely.

We already have a One World Government in place called the UN, and the one world court already in session. We are now watching the assembly of the One World Religion forming in accordance with places like Revelation 17 and 18. It appears

ter of time now before someone like the Vatican an-
s that extraterrestrials are here to help save us from
destructive ways. This will unravel religion as we know it
d my best Holy Spirit-educated guess here is at some point
it will be announced that the Lord Jesus was actually genetically modified and engineered by extraterrestrials.

This will be part of the great end-time deception that will
use all the compelling evidence of science to try and rationally
explain away all the miracles of the Holy Scriptures. For example, that ETs actually parted the Red Sea for Moses and were
helping behind the scenes in every miracle recorded. Let's not
forget 2 Thessalonians 2:10-11, *"And with all deceivableness
of unrighteousness in them that perish; because they received
not the love of the truth, that they might be saved. And for this
cause God shall send them strong delusion, that they should
believe a lie:"*

Recently, scientists confirmed there was no detectable DNA
from a father found in the blood on the face cloth—the sudari-
um—of Jesus Christ of Nazareth (the cloth that wrapped Jesus
head for burial)—only the DNA of the Virgin Mary! Another
recent discovery was that of a death certificate imprinted on
the Shroud of Turin. It stated "This is indeed Jesus Christ of
Nazareth." Hallelujah! Christ has risen and we even have the
physical proof for every doubting Thomas.

Just as Papa God delivered Israel on the first Passover and
brought them out and made them fruitful, the Lord brought
deliverance to the nations at Passover through the sacrifice
of His Son. The mercy, grace and love of God throughout the
entire Bible is to heal and restore. Therefore, let us go now and
be a blessing to everyone you meet in Jesus' name.

Amos 3:7 *"Surely the Lord GOD will do nothing, but he re-
vealeth his secret unto his servants the prophets."*

The events happening in Israel right now will also affect all
the rest of us. Consider this passage that speaks of a time of
trouble in the land of Israel:

Jeremiah 30:6-7 *"Ask ye now, and see whether a man doth
travail with child? wherefore do I see every man with his hands
on his loins, as a woman in travail, and all faces are turned
into paleness? Alas! for that day is great so that none is like it:*

it is even the time of Jacob's trouble, but he shall be saved out of it."

The image of men with their hands on their loins paints a picture of the most horrible tribulation upon a nation. Every nation has much to repent of before the Lord. However, these verses parallel the beginning of sorrows spoken of by Jesus in Matthew 24:8. The time of Jacob's Trouble, also called the Day of the Lord, is certainly coming.

2 Thessalonians 2:1-3 *"Now we beseech you, brethren, by the coming of our Lord Jesus Christ, and by our gathering together unto him, ²That ye be not soon shaken in mind, or be troubled, neither by spirit, nor by word, nor by letter as from us, as that the day of Christ is at hand. ³Let no man deceive you by any means: for that day shall not come, except there come a falling away first, and that man of sin be revealed, the son of perdition;*"

Some Christians are hoping for a great revival before the end. That may be, however, this verse says there will be a falling away first and then the man of sin will be revealed. The antichrist is not revealed until something has been removed.

2 Thessalonians 2:7 *"For the mystery of iniquity doth already work: only he who now letteth will let, until he be taken out of the way.*"

The verse tells us "he" is presently preventing the antichrist from coming forward. That same "he" will be removed. The Church is in the way right now, but one day, we will be gone and there will be no one to hinder him. We will already be with the Lord. The only voices that confront the antichrist are the two witnesses written about in Revelation 11.

This rapture happens in the upheaval of nations described in Ezekiel 38. In the midst of this first gathering of nations, he that restrains—the Church—is removed so the man of sin can be revealed. Maybe that revealing will come as a "special alert" from the media telling how a fleet of UFOs took all the Christians away—and now the world can have real peace and implement their new world order.

Today we are seeing two movements in Christianity, one part is genuine faithful believers, and the other part is a counterfeit version—and within the counterfeit version are those who embrace anything supernatural as being of God.

2 Timothy 4:3-4 *"For the time will come when they will not endure sound doctrine; but after their own lusts shall they heap to themselves teachers, having itching ears; ⁴And they shall turn away their ears from the truth, and shall be turned unto fables."*

The Bible can be utterly trusted. Many of its prophetic messages have already come true. No other books or predictions can compare! The Old Testament—written over a 1,000year period—refers more than 300 times to the coming Messiah. All were fulfilled by Jesus Christ of Nazareth. By that alone, His credentials are established. So I write in great confidence of the prophetic warnings that explain how things will play out before His return.

Matthew 24:24 *"For there shall arise false Christs, and false prophets, and shall shew great signs and wonders; insomuch that, if it were possible, they shall deceive the very elect."*

There are plenty of false christs and false signs and wonders happening right now. Know this one thing: if you are still in a mortal body after you see "Jesus Christ" in the air, or anywhere else for that matter, you are being deceived. The Scripture makes it quite clear that in the nanosecond when we see the Lord Jesus Christ, we will no longer be inhabiting our mortal bodies. We shall be changed.

1 Corinthians 15:51-52 *"Behold, I shew you a mystery; We shall not all sleep, but we shall all be changed, In a moment, in the twinkling of an eye, at the last trump: for the trumpet shall sound, and the dead shall be raised incorruptible, and we shall be changed."*

There are plenty of professing believers engaging in all sorts of paganised practices and doctrines that do not line up with Holy Scriptures. The great deception is in place so it's just a matter of time before something earthshaking occurs, perhaps a nuclear exchange. Is this what Mark 13:20 infers? *"And except that the Lord had shortened those days, no flesh should be saved: but for the elect's sake, whom he hath chosen, he hath shortened the days."*

The Prophets Describe Nuclear War

Papa God gave us prophecy for a good reason and that is to help us prepare ourselves for what the future will bring. The book of Zechariah, written 2,500 years ago in 520 BC seems to describe a future nuclear exchange in rather vivid detail. The prophet gives an account of flying cylinders (rolls, or scrolls) that deliver devastating firepower. They are made of extremely heavy metal, fly across the face of the Earth and consume houses and buildings, leaving a residue behind it that causes massive destruction.

Zechariah even gives the exact dimensions of these flying cylinders, how they are designated, and who is targeted. He wrote this down in a language most don't speak today. I want to explore some of this in Hebrew so we can glean a clearer picture of what is being said.

Zech. 5:1 *"Then I turned, and lifted up mine eyes, and looked, and behold a flying roll."*

What kind of flying roll? This is not a food or pastry roll. In the Strong's number H4039 we find the Hebrew word megillah, which means a roll, book, or writing in a single cylinder. This is not like the Torah, which is wrapped up into with two cylinders. There are ancient copies of the Book of Esther on a single megillah.

Zech. 5:2 *"And he said unto me, What seest thou? And I answered, I see a flying roll; the length thereof is twenty cubits, and the breadth thereof ten cubits."*

The word "breadth" here is not diameter, but it describes a line cast about the circumference. It is like 1 Kings where King Saul is building a house with huge pillars that had a breadth of 30 cubits.

1 Kings 7:6 *"And he made a porch of pillars; the length thereof was fifty cubits, and the breadth thereof thirty cubits: and the porch was before them: and the other pillars and the thick beam were before them."*

The "breadth thereof thirty cubits" was probably not diameter, but the line cast about. The cylinder Zechariah is describing as a megillah works out to be approximately 34.3 feet long, and 5.5 feet in diameter; or 10 cubits/ 3.14 = 3.184 cubits or 5.467 feet wide.

Zech. 5:3-4 *"Then said he unto me, This is the curse that goeth forth over the face of the whole earth: for every one that stealeth shall be cut off as on this side according to it; and ev-*

ery one that sweareth shall be cut off as on that side according to it. I will bring it forth, saith the LORD of hosts, and it shall enter into the house of the thief, and into the house of him that sweareth falsely by my name: and it shall remain in the midst of his house, and shall consume it with the timber thereof and the stones thereof."

This sounds like a nuclear residue or contamination remaining in the midst of the house after it has been consumed.

Zech. 5:5 *"Then the angel that talked with me went forth, and said unto me, Lift up now thine eyes, and see what is this that goeth forth."*

I would imagine the prophet Zachariah knew what a megillah was, as he must have read them often as he studied the Word of God, however, this is something new to him that only looked like a flying megillah.

Zech. 5:6 *"And I said, What is it? And he said, This is an ephah that goeth forth. He said moreover, This is their resemblance through all the earth".*

This ephah is a cylinder container that is filled with 40 liters of some kind. Wouldn't, "their resemblance through all the earth," mean there are many of them throughout the entire earth?

Zech. 5:7 *"And, behold, there was lifted up a talent of lead: and this is a woman that sitteth in the midst of the ephah."*

I discovered that Ishshah is Hebrew for "women," and some think this ephah means "a basket," or in Hebrew some spelling is eyphah with a y. Sometimes words can have more than one meaning, and is the case here. Ishshah can also mean "fire offering," Strong's H801 (maybe if you could combine them that was a foreshadowing of a fiery Irishwoman, whose says, "If it's a fight you're looking for, ye found it!" No, just joking!)

Eyphah, Strong's H374, is a dry measure of quantity equal to 3 seahs, 10 omers; the same as liquid measure bath; about 40 liters. Obviously, this is not about a woman sitting in a basket. This is about a metal cycler that can hold about 40 liters or 10.57 gallons.

The Bible translators of 1601 had no way to imagine and describe in English what we are experiencing in the world today. The way they rendered these verses and information probably did not make a lot of sense to them at that time, either; i.e., "An evil women in a basket with a lead covering." But since 1945, this Hebrew word took on new meaning in the nuclear age. Does this sound like a missile?

A flying megillah can also have writing on the sides, which could be a written curse. "Then said he unto me, This is the curse that goeth forth over the face of the whole earth." Wherever it goes, it kills people by exploding and destroying their homes and buildings—timber and stones—and leaving behind what something that could be radiation. As we read in verse 3 and 4 "and it shall remain in the midst of his house, and shall consume it with the timber thereof and the stones thereof."

Does this flying cylinder contain a thermonuclear warhead?

Zech. 5:8 *"And he said, This is wickedness. And he cast it into the midst of the ephah; and he cast the weight of lead upon the mouth thereof."*

When America took out Hiroshima in WWII, they used a process that could be what is described in Zechariah. Consider this: nuclear fission released the binding energy in certain nuclei. The energy release split the bomb into two roughly equal-mass fragments that imploded into each other. This caused a nuclear explosion. Zechariah says he cast the weight of the lead upon the mouth thereof—or the trigger.

Zech. 5:9 *"Then lifted I up mine eyes, and looked, and, behold, there came out two women, and the wind was in their wings; for they had wings like the wings of a stork: and they lifted up the ephah between the earth and the heaven."*

The flying rolls are sent in judgment. This is the only account in the Bible of women with wings who represent the devil. One must ask, why do we have all these figures and pictures of female angels? Who brought us the idea that angels were females? With "wind in their wings" they flew in the upper atmosphere. Zechariah may have used the word "stork" because he didn't have the words "atomic bomb" in his ancient vocabulary.

Zech. 5:10 *"Then said I to the angel that talked with me, Whither do these bear the ephah?"*

Strong's H374 says this: ephah or eyphah is a receptacle.

Zech. 5:11 *"And he said unto me, To build it an house in the land of Shinar: and it shall be established, and set there upon her own base."*

To build means "to establish, to rebuild" or "to continue in something." The phrase "house" could mean house of sheol or "house of hell" in Hebrew. "Set" is the word yanach, which means to lay down or deposit. "There upon her own base" is mekunah, meaning "resting place."

This is a picture of a fire offering that causes great devastation. It is a round heavy weight of metal (translated "lead") in a 40 liter container. There was no Hebrew word for Uranium 235, so Zechariah describes this as lead. He wasn't wrong, because uranium turns into lead through radioactive decay, and nuclear warheads are typically incased in lead.

The prophet Isaiah describes the effects of this curse.

Isaiah 24:3-6 *"The land shall be utterly emptied, and utterly spoiled: for the LORD hath spoken this word. ⁴The earth mourneth and fadeth away, the world languisheth and fadeth away, the haughty people of the earth do languish. ⁵The earth also is defiled under the inhabitants thereof; because they have transgressed the laws, changed the ordinance, broken the everlasting covenant. ⁶Therefore hath the curse devoured the earth, and they that dwell therein are desolate: therefore the inhabitants of the earth are burned, and few men left.*

Identifying the Mother of Harlots

How passionate should we be to win people to Jesus, understanding these prophecies?

We must learn to imitate the Lord so we can do this and greater things in Jesus name according to places like John 14:12, *"Verily, verily, I say unto you, He that believeth on me, the works that I do shall he do also; and greater works than these shall he do; because I go unto my Father."*

Attitudes are contagious, and the mirror neurons I described earlier are so powerful, we are often reflecting each other's attitudes and intentions whether we mean to or not. If we are children of God, we should act like it and reflect Christ's mercy, grace, and love.

Galatians 6:2 *"Bear ye one another's burdens, and so fulfil the law of Christ."*

We are watching and waiting as the world stage is set for what the Lord warned us would take place. Consider Psalm 83:4: "They have said, Come, and let us cut them off from being a nation; that the name of Israel may be no more in remembrance." Israel is presently surrounded by Arab states. Their Islamic leaders have made their intentions to utterly remove the name of Israel from the map. We will soon see an all-out Arab-Israeli war in the Middle East? According to Ezekiel 38, Russia, Iran, Turkey and a number of other countries will invade Israel, but it seems the Arabs will go first and be supernaturally defeated.

In the meantime we see the new Pope Francis recently declared that everyone was redeemed through Jesus, including atheists. He also called Islam a religion of peace, and warned that no one should speak of it being violent.

Galatians 1:8 *"But though we, or an angel from heaven, preach any other gospel unto you than that which we have preached unto you, let him be accursed."*

For those who might be presently embracing a modern message I term "grace on steroids," let's not forget the Mosaic Law which Jesus came to fulfill. The Old Testament is for our instruction in righteousness.

Matthew 5:17 *"Think not that I am come to destroy the law, or the prophets: I am not come to destroy, but to fulfil."*

There are a lot of serious toxic side effects with steroids, they are simply not good for you. In your heart of hearts, if you know steroid abuse can't be good, you need to understand that neither can this popular modern message of Grace of forgiveness, without true repentance be good. Can there be any true salvation without regeneration? Can the Church offer heaven and neglect to explain about the consequences of hell? What good is Christianity if the follower of Jesus is not obeying Him? What will happen to those churches in which pastors and preachers deny the full giftings of the Holy Spirit? Will they also try to remove salvation through Christ and call that which is evil, good, and that which is good, evil?

Isaiah 5:20 *"Woe unto them that call evil good, and good evil; that put darkness for light, and light for darkness; that put bitter for sweet, and sweet for bitter!"*

Just like Jesus, pastors are to warn people of what is to come. Remember, Jesus tried to explain to His disciples that He needed to go into Jerusalem. He told them he would suffer severely. They didn't understand the purpose of the crucifixion or that in His death and resurrection, they would be saved. Peter even tried to stop Jesus, but he said to him, "Get behind me Satan."

Matthew 16:23 *"But he turned, and said unto Peter, Get thee behind me, Satan: thou art an offence unto me: for thou savourest not the things that be of God, but those that be of men. you savorest the things that be of men."*

Papa God wants your love. That means He needs your hearts to be willing to trust Him in everything. The Lord wants us to understand the Scriptures. He wants us to recognize the system that is represented as the woman riding the beast in the Book of Revelation who got drunk with the blood of the saints.

Who is this MOTHER OF HARLOTS AND ABOMINATIONS OF THE EARTH we read in Revelation 17?

Could it be the Vatican? After all, it is the Vatican who owns the LUCIFER telescope in the Mount Graham Observatory in Arizona. It is Vatican astronomers who are observing the faintest and most distant objects in the universe. Why is the Vatican so concerned with astrobiology? Because astrobiology is concerned with the effects of outer space on living organisms, and includes the search for extraterrestrial life. One definition I found interesting was: (1) understanding the conditions under which life can arise, (2) looking for habitable worlds, and (3) searching for evidence of life.

According to the Bible we shall see a charismatic, nice man who signs a peace treaty for Israel. He will come with lying signs and wonders, but how many will be deceived and believe him to be the long-awaited Messiah of the Jews? I dare say only Berean-type individuals (Acts 17:11) will recognize the antichrist.

We read about him in Daniel 11: 37-39: *"Neither shall he regard the God of his fathers, nor the desire of women, nor re-*

gard any god: for he shall magnify himself above all. [This is describing the Antichrist] ³⁸But in his estate shall he honour the God of forces: and a god whom his fathers knew not shall he honour with gold, and silver, and with precious stones, and pleasant things. ³⁹Thus shall he do in the most strong holds with a strange god, whom he shall acknowledge and increase with glory: and he shall cause them to rule over many, and shall divide the land for gain."

He shall honor a god whom his fathers did not know. Could this be an alien god, some kind of demon?

There have been many cultural preparations to condition us to accept an alien antichrist. On September 21, 1987, President Ronald Reagan alluded to this type of scenario in a speech to the UN. He said, "In our obsession with antagonisms of the moment, we often forget how much unites all the members of humanity. Perhaps we need some outside, universal threat to make us recognize this common bond. I occasionally think how quickly our differences worldwide would vanish if we were facing an alien threat from outside this world. And yet, I ask, is not an alien force already among us?"

Perhaps the Pope and his top astrobiologists will reveal that there are other created beings presently interacting with our planet. This will unravel religion as we know it.

The world is already primed to accept these alien visitors as more powerful and more highly evolved, the saviors of mankind. The Bible tells us great multitudes of people will be primed to follow the Antichrist's comprehensive plan of evil.

2 Thessalonians 2:10-11 *"And with all deceivableness of unrighteousness in them that perish; because they received not the love of the truth, that they might be saved. And for this cause God shall send them strong delusion, that they should believe a lie:"*

If something doesn't feel right, sound right, or look right—if it doesn't line up with the Bible— there is a problem that needs to be addressed. When in doubt, cast it out, in the name of Jesus! All this is to be expected because Satan himself masquerades as an angel of light.

2 Corinthians 11:14-15 *"And no marvel; for Satan himself is transformed into an angel of light. and so it shouldn't be surprising, then, if his servants also "masquerade as servants of*

righteousness. Therefore it is no great thing if his ministers also be transformed as the ministers of righteousness; whose end shall be according to their works.".

History has proven time and time again that when mankind tries to live without God, horrid things happen. Christians are being killed every day in various parts of the world. How can we truly think that it can't happen in America?

Revelation 17:6 *"And I saw the woman drunken with the blood of the saints, and with the blood of the martyrs of Jesus: and when I saw her, I wondered with great admiration."*

In the end times, the nation that is Mystery Babylon coming out of Rome will witness the shedding of the blood of the saints. Many now think the Pope is fulfilling the requirements as the false prophet. Let us therefore avoid the mysteries of iniquity and continue to study diligently the great mystery of godliness. Let us be aware of what is unfolding before us prophetically. Let us practice staying in a place of worship and humility that we cultivate a spirit of gratitude in our hearts as we follow Christ our Lord. The more we seek to be like Jesus, the less easily we shall deceived.

Hebrews 11:6 *"But without faith it is impossible to please him: for he that cometh to God must believe that he is, and that he is a rewarder of them that diligently seek him."*

Chapter Nine

GOD'S PROMISES AND COMING TRIBULATIONS

Please recall in Daniel 3 there is a wonderful example of three fellows (Shadrach, Meshach, and Abednego) who understood how to stay in faith. They refused to bow down to evil and were willing to go into the burning fiery furnace. They not only survived certain death in that fire but as they came out they didn't even smell like smoke. Their miraculous survival caused King Nebuchadnezzar to decree that his entire kingdom would now serve the Lord their God.

I tell you the truth, staying in faith in these end times is not just believing God is real and in control (although only you have control over your thought life), staying in faith means trusting the Lord in everything no matter how it might look at any given moment.

James 2:19 *"Thou believest that there is one God; thou doest well: the devils also believe, and tremble. But wilt thou know, O vain man, that faith without works is dead?"*

This means demons certainly acknowledge and believe in God but they remain demons; however, you still have freedom of choice and you can work out your faith.

Philippians 2:12 *"Wherefore, my beloved, as ye have always obeyed, not as in my presence only, but now much more in my absence, work out your own salvation with fear and trembling."*

Who would ever sail on a ship or fly in an airplane if you couldn't trust the captain in charge to get you to your final destination? I dare say you would walk off and find another way to travel. The Lord Jesus did not come just to earth to give us something to believe, but rather somebody we can totally trust. We are to keep looking to Jesus for everything.

Hebrews 12:2 *"Looking unto Jesus the author and finisher of our faith; who for the joy that was set before him endured the cross, despising the shame, and is set down at the right hand of the throne of God."*

In other words, it is more than just uttering some formal statements that truly converts you. It is truly a matter of re-penting of sin and moment-by-moment and learning to trust the Lord. He will supply all of your needs (see Phil. 4:19).

He will supply all your needs—food, clothing, shelter, etc. This means we can focus on sharing Christ's love, healing the sick, and casting out demons in Jesus' name everywhere we go. Besides, the way the biblical prophesies are unfolding so rapidly, we may be caught up together with Christ before these things you are concerned about even happens!

May I remind you of Romans 14:8, *"For whether we live, we live unto the Lord; and whether we die, we die unto the Lord: whether we live therefore, or die, we are the Lord's."*

Now I say all this because we read in Luke 10:2 *"Therefore said he unto them, The harvest truly is great, but the labourers are few: pray ye therefore the Lord of the harvest, that he would send forth labourers into his harvest."*

We are to help bring in a harvest through repentance, deliverance and healing in Jesus' name.

When you look at the church today, why is it we still see practically no difference between her and the secular world? Both are filled with people offending each other, lying and being dishonest about each other, relationships falling apart, marriages fail, financial troubles abound and corruption is everywhere. We feel lost, abandoned, and rejected, as though we are under some sort of curse. Perhaps some are.

Deuteronomy 28:1-2 *"And it shall come to pass, if thou shalt hearken diligently unto the voice of the LORD thy God, to observe and to do all his commandments which I command thee this day, that the LORD thy God will set thee on high above all nations of the earth:" And all these blessings shall come on thee, and overtake thee, if thou shalt hearken unto the voice of the LORD thy God."*

This means blessings shall come to pass only "IF" we will do as the Lord instructs us. In verse 15 we read if we won't obey the Lord's instructions then curses are able to overtake us which includes all sicknesses and diseases and problems of every kind. In fact in verse 61 we find that every sickness and every plague which was not written and listed here is also included. God's nature is to heal and restore, but the devil comes to steal, kill, and destroy.

As a result of not understanding God's Word, too many people are not walking in the blessings and missing the more abundant life Jesus came to bring us. In John chapter 15 Jesus gives us a word picture of Himself as the "Vine," and all His disciples as the branches. As branches of Christ we are to bear good fruit, and enjoy an abundant life. This is more than just believing and having faith—it means we must also act. We read in James 1:22, *"But be ye doers of the word, and not hearers only, deceiving your own selves."*

Does this mean there are people who have heard the gospel truth but for some reason have not acted on it?

Sadly, we see too many people today in the world and in the church, who end up going to see a secular health care professional or psychologist, often ending up on some medication to help deaden the pain which is not getting at the root of the real problem at all. This is like going to see your auto mechanic when your oil light comes on and he solves the problem by simply unhooking the oil light and sends you on your way. Somewhere down the road your motorcar is going to experience a breakdown!

That's why we are instructed to take every thought captive to the obedience of Christ (2 Corinthians 10:5). We must practice godly thinking because not every thought is your own. Some come from the enemy! God has already equipped us to do this, according to 1 Corinthians 2:16 *"For who hath known the mind of the Lord, that he may instruct him? But we have the mind of Christ."*

Philippians 4:13 *"I can do all things through Christ which strengtheneth me."*

If more of us practiced this, we would be seeing the same sorts of results the early Church saw in the book of Acts. We wouldn't need to send so many people to the secular health care professionals because we have real answers for real problems. We would be preaching the whole gospel, healing the sick, and casting out demons in Jesus' name.

The day of Pentecost is celebrated 50 days after Passover. It marks the day the Holy Spirit came as tongues of fire on the disciples. I was invited to speak about this to a gathering of people, mostly from a certain mainstream denomination who believe that some of the gifts of the Holy Spirit stopped operating about 2,000 years ago. As I concluded my message, the power of the Holy Spirit came into that place like it did in the Book of Acts, with signs and wonders following. A number of people received gifts of the Holy Spirit, and the Lord also demonstrated healing miracles, along with prophesy in unknown tongues and interpretations.

I was asked to pray for a young woman at this meeting who was injured in a motorcycle accident. The Lord in His mercy, grace and love healed her instantly. To God be all the glory. The Lord called His disciples to observe what He did and then go and help make more disciples in every generation. He expects us to fulfill scriptures like John 14:12, "Verily, verily, I say unto you, He that believeth on me, the works that I do shall he do also; and greater works than these shall he do; because I go unto my Father."

If Jesus healed and did creative cures because He was anointed by the Holy Ghost as stated in places like Acts 10:38, then He has every right to expect us to do this as well. When the Baptism of the Holy Spirit comes on Christ's disciples, then we are equipped to go into the harvest and complete the great commission to the ends of the earth.

We are facing a time that is unprecedented: the global turmoil that makes World War III a strong possibility, Islam's agenda for world domination, and the threats of an "alien"/ demonic takeover. It seems like many in the church are like the Israelites hiding in the cliff of the rocks, afraid to face the giant. They have forgotten that when you trust the Lord for everything, He will back you up as he did David, or Shadrach,

Meshach, and Abednego. Understand that without faith it is impossible to please God, Romans 14:23. Without faith, you are in fear, which is sin, and God cannot bless you in sin.

I tell you the truth, prayer changes things when we pray in obedience and humbleness before our God and repent of our sins. He give us the Holy Spirit to discern and recognise those places where we have entertained thoughts and ideas from the enemy. Ignorance is not bliss!

2 Chronicles 7:14, *"If my people, which are called by my name, shall humble themselves, and pray, and seek my face, and turn from their wicked ways; then will I hear from heaven, and will forgive their sin, and will heal their land."*

Let's be prepared all the time for His coming, because as Jesus stated in Matthew 24:42-44, *"Watch therefore: for ye know not what hour your Lord doth come. ⁴³But know this, that if the goodman of the house had known in what watch the thief would come, he would have watched, and would not have suffered his house to be broken up. ⁴⁴Therefore, be ye also ready: for in such an hour as ye think not the Son of man cometh."*

Let's further prepare ourselves by considering the following conditions for the end times from Mark 13:6-9:

1. Many Antichrists will come

Mark 13:6 *"For many shall come in my name, saying, I am Christ; and shall deceive many."*

There are several men claiming to be Jesus Christ today in several nations and some have large followings. I wonder what it would be like to get them all into one conference together.

When he shows up, the Antichrist will bring a faulty peace plan that will be used to destroy many people. The antichrist will make some sort of promise to the world, like politicians regularly do, and the world will believe him. He will even convince Israel he has a workable peace agreement; all they need to do is follow him. Mind you, what appears like good intentions will turn into such extreme evil it will make the Nazis seem like Boy Scouts.

Read this

2. There will be wars and rumours of wars, earthquakes, famines, and troubles

Mark 13:7-8 *"And when ye shall hear of wars and rumours of wars, be ye not troubled: for such things must needs be; but the end shall not be yet. For nation shall rise against nation, and kingdom against kingdom: and there shall be earthquakes in divers places, and there shall be famines and troubles: these are the beginnings of sorrows."*

There are wars or rumblings in nearly every corner of the world. Each day seems to bring more news of domestic attacks, American against American, bombings, attacks by men in trucks, men armed with axes and other unspeakable horrors. Muslim nations are not exempt, as Sunnis fight Shias and Saudi kingdoms rise up against each other.

There are reports of earthquakes, famines, and diseases. These are called the beginnings of sorrows, which also mark the beginning of the second half of the seven-year tribulation.

3. Christians will be Persecuted

Mark 13:9 *"But take heed to yourselves: for they shall deliver you up to councils; and in the synagogues ye shall be beaten: and ye shall be brought before rulers and kings for my sake, for a testimony against them."*

Christians are losing their lives at the hands of terrorists. They are given a choice by ISIS and its offshoot organizations to convert to Islam or die. This is actually commanded in the Q'uran. Non-Muslims are often beaten and taken before tribal leaders; some are publicly humiliated and recorded before being executed.

4. Every nation will be aware of the gospel.

Mark 13:10 *"And the gospel must first be published among all nations."*

We have the Internet, Facebook and other social media, television, radio, Internet radio, etc. The Bible has been translated in every single language and is accessible to everyone today. I dare say that the gospel has now pretty much reached the entire world. The good news of salvation through Jesus Christ must be preached to all so that no one can claim they didn't understand. Papa God desires for all to be saved, but He will not go against our free will. He also is not waiting for the last person to be saved before the rapture, because many shall be saved after the rapture.

Preparing by Prayer with Thanksgiving

As we approach this time, let us continue to pray that the sleeping church wakes up and takes action instead of rolling over and going back to sleep. Let us be thankful now, for it is the will of God and that has never changed.

1 Thessalonias 5:18 *"In every thing give thanks: for this is the will of God in Christ Jesus concerning you."*

It is easy be thankful when things are going jolly well in your relationships, health and business. But when times are difficult and challenging, we often get focused on what the devil is doing rather than what God has done for us and is doing.

We read in Psalm 106:1 *"Praise ye the Lord. O give thanks unto the Lord; for he is good: for his mercy endureth for ever."*

Notice this verse does not say to give thanks to the Lord only when you're feeling good! Rather, it says, "Give thanks to the Lord, for He is good."

So what do we do when we feel overwhelmed with all these evil things unfolding in this fallen world? We must overcome those thoughts and feelings by worshipping the Lord in prayer, praise ant thanksgiving. We read in Hebrews 13:15, *"By him therefore let us offer the sacrifice of praise to God continually, that is, the fruit of our lips giving thanks to his name."*

We're commanded to give thanks regardless of circumstances, and to raise our voices in thanks to God. What if a parent never told their children verbally how much they loved them, or a husband just assumed his wife knows she is loved and never actually tells her? That brings in all sorts of issues and opens gateways to the wrong kingdom. At salvation, we spoke a confession out of our mouth, so it is the same when we bless and thank the Lord.

A Final Warning From God

Let me conclude with 1 Thessalonians 5:1-28:

¹But of the times and the seasons, brethren, ye have no need that I write unto you. This is referring to the Rapture.

²For yourselves know perfectly that the day of the Lord so cometh as a thief in the night.

³For when they shall say, Peace and safety; then sudden destruction cometh upon them, as travail upon a woman with child; and they shall not escape.

⁴But ye, brethren, are not in darkness, that that day should overtake you as a thief. We are to watch and pray at all times for the return of the Lord.

⁵Ye are all the children of light, and the children of the day: we are not of the night, nor of darkness. Christians shall escape this sudden destruction.

⁶Therefore let us not sleep, as do others; but let us watch and be sober. Let us meet the conditions to escape these things by living holy lives.

⁷For they that sleep, sleep in the night; and they that be drunken are drunken in the night.

⁸But let us, who are of the day, be sober, putting on the breastplate of faith and love; and for an helmet, the hope of salvation.

⁹For God hath not appointed us to wrath, but to obtain salvation by our Lord Jesus Christ, Right here the Lord tells us it is not appointed for Christians to go through the tribulation wrath and sudden destruction.

¹⁰Who died for us, that, whether we wake or sleep, we should live together with him. We as disciples in Christ, dead or alive, will be raptured and live with Christ forever, escaping the wrath that is coming.

¹¹Wherefore comfort yourselves together, and edify one another, even as also ye do.

¹²And we beseech you, brethren, to know them which labour among you, and are over you in the Lord, and admonish you;

[13]*And to esteem them very highly in love for their work's sake. And be at peace among yourselves. Ministers of the gospel are not only to be respected, but esteemed as well.*

[14]*Now we exhort you, brethren, warn them that are unruly, comfort the feebleminded, support the weak, be patient toward all men. Pray for those unruly ones who are out of step and not performing their duty to the Lord and church.*

[15]*See that none render evil for evil unto any man; but ever follow that which is good, both among yourselves, and to all men. This means you must be willing to forgive all offenses and walk in Christ's love continually. As soon as you forgive others and yourself, you enter into holiness before the Lord.*

[16]*Rejoice evermore. If you connect with the awesome love of God, how can you not rejoice evermore?*

[17]*Pray without ceasing. Prayers make a difference.*

[18]*In every thing give thanks: for this is the will of God in Christ Jesus concerning you. God's will for your life is that you maintain an attitude of gratitude before Christ.*

[19]*Quench not the Spirit.*

[20]*Despise not prophesyings. How many churches today will allow someone to share a prophecy or speak in an unknown tongue with interpretation? Most churches will have the ushers escort you out of the building if you try to share what the Lord is showing you. What a sad reality, but it shows how far have we have drifted from the Word of God.*

[21]*Prove all things; hold fast that which is good.*

[22]*Abstain from all appearance of evil. In other words, "Follow peace with all men, and holiness, without which no man shall see the Lord, Hebrews 12:14.*

[23]*And the very God of peace sanctify you wholly; and I pray God your whole spirit and soul and body be preserved blameless unto the coming of our Lord Jesus Christ. (God wants you blessed and your whole body in health.*

[24]*Faithful is he that calleth you, who also will do it. If God said it, we are to believe it. God will never lie to us, whereas the devil is the father of lies.*

²⁵Brethren, pray for us. Instead of complaining about those in leadership, you ought to be praying for them.

²⁶Greet all the brethren with an holy kiss. How many are willing to do this today?

²⁷I charge you by the Lord that this epistle be read unto all the holy brethren. This is for us today.

²⁸The grace of our Lord Jesus Christ be with you. Amen. Surely Paul understood the grace of God and the limitations of that grace for those who refuse to obey the Lord.

Now consider this: The Lord Jesus took some of the most unlikely people and did great things through them. He made disciples out of some smelly uneducated fisherman who He empowered and commissioned to go heal the sick, raise the dead, and cleanse the lepers. Then He sent out the 70, just as we are sent out today.

When the disciples said to Jesus, *"Send these people away into the villages so they can find something to eat."* Jesus said, *"You will feed them."* And as the scriptures tell us, they took give loaves of bread and two fishes and fed more than 5,000 men—perhaps 10,000 including women and children. They ate until they were all filled, and afterwards the disciples collected 12 baskets filled up with leftovers. Jesus had compassion on everyone there and He healed all who were sick (see Matthew 14:13-21).

Jesus healed a paralyzed man and commanded him *"Take up your bed and walk."* He commanded the corpse of a young man to come back to life and presented him alive to his mother (see Luke 7:11-17).

Jesus told his friend who was entombed four days in a grave to come forth. Lazarus' spirit obeyed, reentered his body, and walked out of the tomb. Jesus told Peter to come and Peter walked on the water. All these simply did what Jesus said to do. Jesus commands the impossible and then makes it possible, because all things are possible with Him. He is the same yesterday today and forever. That's why we as true disciples cannot lose. Again, I remind you of Romans 14:8 *"For whether we live, we live unto the Lord; and whether we die, we die unto the Lord: whether we live therefore, or die, we are the Lord's."*

So keep your joy and keep your peace and let us help bring in the end time Harvest.

Chapter Ten

A FINAL EXPOSURE ON FEAR VS. FAITH

Some may find the spirit of fear troubling them after reading these things. Let me explain how to overcome it—whether you're fearful of these end-time issues, or have other fears, such about finances, relationships, unsaved loved ones, etc.

Our minds were designed to analyze information and be triggered by previous memories. We generate between 30,000 to 70,000 thoughts a day. Some of them are from your own thinking, some are Godinspired, and others have been projected into your mind by the devil. Do you suppose there are some evil-inspired thoughts that you blindly accepted and then realised later were toxic? There is a point to which these thoughts can become spiritually, emotionally and physically dangerous.

Thoughts that come as a feeling or impression of fear, stress and anxiety are like a Trojan horse, filled with warriors who work against you. By entertaining them, you open the gates for an invasion! Your body can only secrete chemicals and hormones in response to what you are thinking: if you are entertaining fear, then your body chemistry will reflect those fearful thoughts. I believe every attack of fear that isn't challenged by the truth from God's Word is counterproductive to your health. When you "lose" your peace mentally and spiritually, then you may be allowing sickness and diseases to come in physically.

My friend Dr. Michelle Strydom shared some amazing insights with me about how our kidneys and adrenal glands help us in decision making. Research is showing that both your heart as well as your kidneys act like a minibrain in your body. The word "reins" in the Old Testament literally means kidneys and adrenal glands in the original Hebrew of the text.

Psalm 26:2 *"Examine me, O LORD, and prove me; try my reins and my heart."*

Psalm 139:13 *"For thou hast possessed my reins: thou hast covered me in my mother's womb."*

The left kidney assesses the situations you are in, and then based on how the situation is framed by the left kidney, the right kidney devises a strategy to move forward. If the left kidney assesses the situation badly, for example not completely trusting the Lord, the right kidney is then not able to resolve things properly. The result is that the kidneys end up releasing stress hormones into your blood stream.

Consider Proverbs 13:12 *"Hope deferred maketh the heart sick: but when the desire cometh, it is a tree of life."*

When we are tormented by spirits of fear and hopelessness, we can become heartsick. Is it any wonder that heart disease is one of the leading causes of death? However, if you face every situation trusting the Lord, even when you don't know how things shall work out, the kidneys will release DHEA molecule—which carries the emotion of joy—and your heart then releases ANH (atrial natriuretic hormone) which carries the emotion of peace. This helps bring about healing spiritually, emotionally and physically. After putting your trust in Jesus/ Yeshua, it brings you supernatural peace.

John 14:27 *"Peace I leave with you, my peace I give unto you: not as the world giveth, give I unto you. Let not your heart be troubled, neither let it be afraid."*

Why would any true believer ever doubt the Word of God? Why wouldn't you simply doubt the lies of the demons who gave you such imaginative thoughts instead? God means what He says and He said what He means. The moment you decide to doubt the lies of the devil and simply believe God, you begin to connect and receive guidance from the Holy Spirit. Entering into a place of faith can literally move those mountains the spirit of doubt and unbelief built.

Mark 11:23 *"For verily I say unto you, that whosoever shall say unto this mountain, Be thou removed and be thou cast into the sea, and shall not doubt in his heart, But shall believe that those things which he saith shall come to pass, He shall have whatsoever he saith."*

My educated guess here is that most people who read this passage probably gloss over the literal meaning about moving mountains. Not very many people appear to understand or truly imagine how beliefs and words can actually move mountains.

Simon the Tanner

There is an amazing account from the tenth century of a peasant called Simon the Tanner or Saint Simon the Shoemaker, who moved a mountain to avoid persecution by the Muslims. He lived in Cairo, Egypt under a Muslim ruler. The ruler found the New Testament verse in which Jesus declared, *"If ye have faith as a grain of mustard seed, ye shall say unto this mountain, remove hence to yonder place; and it shall remove; and nothing shall be impossible unto you"* (Matthew 17:20), and demanded that the Christians prove it. Mokattam Mountain was was spoiling the view from his palace, and he commanded that they move it. If their religion proved powerless, and the mountain stayed in place, he would kill all the Christians in the village.

Simon believed the Word of God, and when he commanded the mountain to move, a great earthquake shook the area. Each time he and his fellow Christians stood up to worship the eternal living Christ, the mountain was lifted upwards. Eventually, the sun could be seen shining underneath it! When the people sat down, the mountain thrust down, it is recorded this happened three times before the mountain was moved and set down several miles away. Needless to say, the Christian community was saved. Interestingly, it was said that Simon was never seen again. Some believed that he disappeared to avoid receiving any glory or credit for the miracle. He still is beloved today by Christians, as well as many Muslims. There is a church built in the place where the mountain moved to commemorate this miracle, with carvings and paintings to depict the event.

Is it so hard to believe that God can do the same sorts of things today? Someone sent me a recent testimony of a young boy with severe asthma issues for whom the doctors could do nothing. They sent him home, and he died on the way. When his mother saw that he was dead, she wanted to die herself. In that village it was not permissible to bury the dead that particular day, so the boy's body was laid on the ground and family and friends mourned his passing.

Then Doctor Messiah Jesus showed up—working through a traveling evangelist. The man boldly professed that Jesus would raise the boy back to life. The villagers wondered how could this happen when the boy has been dead 24 hours, but the evangelist showed them videos of miracles and they had faith to believe it could happen, and it did. What's more, his asthma was gone! After the boy came back to life, his doctor became a Christian, as did many others. Even the villagers turned from their false religions to a belief in Christ.

Faith to move a mountain starts with simple faith and grows when we offer thanksgiving, praise, and worship to God. When you thank the Lord, He listens, and when you praise His Holy name, He is by your side. The angel of the Lord encamps round you, and when you worship, Christ acts on your behalf!

What about when we have been programmed in unbelief and doubt? These are strong holds of toxic thoughts, strengthened by bad decisions. Let's consider them mountains of ungodly thinking. God has designed our brain in such a way that we are able to stand outside of ourselves and look at what's going on in our mind to gain proper perspective. We need to observe the toxic thoughts as mountains and command them to move. Then, we shall replace them with healthy thoughts. This all takes practice, as does anything worthwhile. Keep your focus on the outcome! If you align yourself in the Word of God, you can crowd out those toxic thoughts that you once obeyed.

Now when you speak to the mountains, people around you—including other believers who don't know the Word of God—may criticize and ridicule you. They did the same to the evangelist before the dead boy was resurrected. What if he listened to those scoffers and doubters instead of the Holy Spirit? That boy would have been buried now and long gone, instead of being alive and experiencing the power of the living God in him.

Remember, the key is to follow 2 Corinthians 10:5 and take all your thoughts captive to the obedience of Christ.

The Atomic Power of Faith

Atoms are the building blocks of everything in our universe, and exist on the borderline between the existent and the non-existent. We should apply this concept to everything else the Lord has made, since each is simply a large collection of atoms in various arrangements. The idea of atoms has been known since the ancient Greeks. For ages, people thought the atom was the smallest thing that could not be divided. Then back in the mid1930s, atoms were discovered to have been made up of three fundamental particles: protons, neutrons and electrons. The Bible sums it this way in Colossians 1:17, *"And he is before all things, and by him all things consist."*

The Lord Jesus was born or begotten before all creation, and before any creature was ever made, according to His pleasure, and for His praise and glory.

Revelation 4:11 *"Thou art worthy, O Lord, to receive glory and honour and power: for thou hast created all things, and for thy pleasure they are and were created."*

A substance is something you can measure. The Bible also says that our faith, hope and belief is substance that can be measured, literally, *"Now faith is the substance of things hoped for, the evidence of things not seen"* (Hebrews 11:1).

Our words are sound waves that impact the physical world. If we kept these things in mind, we would be a whole lot more careful about what we thought, said, or did.

Now, let's think of mountains in the same way, and then it's not so difficult to imagine how our faith and words can move them. God has given us instructions on how:

Romans 10:17 *"So then faith cometh by hearing, and hearing by the word of God."*

Hebrews 11:6 *"But without faith it is impossible to please him: for he that cometh to God must believe that he is, and that he is a rewarder of them that diligently seek him."*

The invisible particles that form dust and rocks are atoms. The particles of disease are things like viruses and germs. And just like we cannot see these particles, we do not comprehend the spirit world with our eyes. That is, unless you put it under God's microscope and begin to discern things such as spirits of fear, spirits of infirmity, and so on.

Scientists are now saying that the simplest objects in the universe are actually shaped like strings. Each basic particle is created by the strings vibrating in different patterns. Albert Einstein showed us how a solid object of energy is only different from fluid forms of energy in the rate at which the atoms are moving. This was his famous equation, E = MC2. Solid matter accelerated to a very high rate of speed becomes pure energy.

Water takes different forms depending on how fast its atoms are moving—at low levels of energy it is ice, but as the water molecules vibrate more rapidly, the ice melts. If the molecules are really boosted, water turns into steam. With our eyes we may see frozen ice cubes, but even with our limited understanding we know that ice can change to water or into steam and appear to evaporate. In essence, we are using 'faith' when we turn on the stove to boil water.

Likewise, we could say the things we can see are simply made up of things that we cannot see, and there is an invisible reality behind what we can see in the natural. For believers in Christ, this is where knowledge and faith come together. As it says in Hebrews 4:13, *"Neither is there any creature that is not manifest in his sight: but all things are naked and opened unto the eyes of him with whom we have to do."*

When you think, that thought actually receives an invitation or signal that moves it from your unconscious mind into the conscious part of your mind. The activity of thinking takes up actual space in your brain, and by principles of quantum physics, we know there is a real force behind it. This force involves particle-like and wavelike interactions of energy and matter.

Researchers in field of quantum physics are observing things that defy the laws of physics of what was once understood. These studies show that particles have strange and unexpected qualities about them. Let's face it, we serve a supernatural God where all things are possible with Him. I think the Lord may have designed science as a way of showing just how awesome all His creation is!

Even when we look at the mountains of problems in the world today, we know there is hope with the Lord. As you look at the mountains in your own life, see them as a Christian ought to see them. Look at them with the eyes of your understanding, not just with your physical eyes. We walk by faith, not by sight.

If we stay in the Word of God so the Word of God stays in us, it seems we eventually start to see a literal mountain as nothing more than a vibrating mass of invisible particles. The Lord Jesus told us that what we believe can move a mountain. We activate our faith—the substance of things hoped for, the evidence of things not seen—understanding it is a powerful spiritual principle. If faith is a real substance, that means that our beliefs have weight and affect, not only on our bodies, but also on invisible realities. Have you ever entered a room and felt the energy coming from someone either in a positive or negative way? Jesus did not do any mighty works in His home town of Nazareth. He was only able to heal a few people because they did not believe He was who He said He was.

You will see a change in your life if you begin to comprehend faith as substance. We know that everyone believes in something—why not believe and take comfort in what God promises.

Matthew 21:22 *"And all things, whatsoever ye shall ask in prayer, believing, ye shall receive."*

Jesus brought a little girl back to life because of her father's faith. He said, "Be not afraid, only believe." How many times did Jesus heal someone and tell them, "Thy faith hath made thee whole?" Faith and belief are at the centre of our being, and so powerful they can actually change DNA. Beliefs are not just what we think about and agree with, they are those things that we are so convinced of they affect us emotionally, spiritually, and physically.

All through the Holy Scriptures there is this theme of instruction on the importance of believing God at His Word. Anyone seeking the Lord for anything shall find Him. If you need physical healing, best to start recognising that spirit fear and doubt that is telling you God will bless others but somehow you are disqualified. Likewise, meditating on healing scriptures day and night will heal all your flesh (see Proverbs 4:22). Getting before the Lord and feeling the joy in your heart that

He saved you is a good starting place. Your words reflect and activate your faith. Instead of saying you're struggling, say you're overcoming.

Deuteronomy 4:29 *"But if from thence thou shalt seek the LORD thy God, thou shalt find him, if thou seek him with all thy heart and with all thy soul."*

In Mark 11:23 the Lord Jesus gives us the connection between speaking and believing, "But shall believe in his heart that what he saith will come to pass, he will have what he saith."

The Lord wants you healthy and He tells us so in 3 John 2, *"Beloved, I wish above all things that thou mayest prosper and be in health, even as thy soul prospereth."*

Again, we must always ask ourselves, "Am I submitting every thought to the obedience of Christ?" Every thought should have to pass this test: Is this good for me to think and dwell on and does it please the Lord, or is it harmful and does it please the devil?

One way to tell if your thoughts are lies from the devil or truth from the Lord is to simply add "in Jesus' name" after each thought. For example, if you were to hear yourself say," I am such a reject no one really cares for me, in Jesus' name." It's rather obvious which kingdom this toxic thought comes from! It needs to be cast out. Likewise, if we add "in Jesus' name" after a positive thought, it will harmonise with the Word God and within our spirits. For example, "I am the apple of His eye, in Jesus' name." Now, that is truth!

The Lord Jesus said in Luke 11:34-36, *"The light of the body is the eye: therefore when thine eye is single, thy whole body also is full of light; but when thine eye is evil, thy body also is full of darkness. Take heed therefore that the light which is in thee be not darkness. If thy whole body therefore be full of light, having no part dark, the whole shall be full of light, as when the bright shining of a candle doth give thee light."*

The words you speak shall shape your world because they are designed with creative ability. In fact, what you confess over yourself is what you will become. For it is written Proverbs 18:21, *"Death and life are in the power of the tongue: and they that love it shall eat the fruit thereof."*

Proverbs 23:7a *"For as he thinketh in his heart, so is he."*

Your response in emotions are simply a product of your thought life. If your thoughts are good, healthy, positive and godly, so shall your emotions be. Your body will obey and you shall stay in homeostasis—which is a medical term for health and balance. If you entertain unclean spirits by thinking like they do, how do you expect to stay healthy? Your body can only follow the orders you give it. My point here is that your will and emotions are part of your mind. We can understand now from 3 John 2 that your life and health is an expression of your thoughts. Think about that!

The simple message of Jesus' love for mankind, and His simple offer of salvation can be drowned out by spirits of confusion. Who are we to believe? Shall we look to the media or folks in the entertainment industry to protect us from what is to come—or shall we trust in the Lord?

How to Begin a Relationship with the Lord

The Lord Jesus loves you more than you could ever know, and He loves you exactly as you are right now. He wants to bless and heal you! Jesus even loves those who have been programmed to hate Him. The Lord extends mercy, grace and love to all people great and small, of every colour and race, to all genders and sexual orientations. For we have all sinned and come short of His glory and we all desperately need Him.

He wants to be a part of your life right now. Does that mean you will have to make some changes? Yes. There are things in all of our lives that need to change.

You have probably heard it said that Jesus approves of all lifestyles. Some will say because He hung out with tax-collectors and prostitutes, that means He approves. On the contrary, Jesus asks us to repent and turn away from dead works—the things that cause damage in our lives and don't line up with His design for us. Throughout history, Jesus has been making changes in people's lives—and it's always for the better. We can read the accounts of people like Zacchaeus, who basically was trying to get rich off of others, the woman caught in prostitution, and others who were healed by Him, then told to stop sinning.

The world does not like the word sin—in fact there is a great movement—even in Christianity —to eradicate the concept of sin. The demonically charged plans of people like Aleister Crowley seem to be taking shape. He famously said, "Do What Thou Wilt," which has become "do what you want, where you want, and how you want." There is an egotistical quest for instant gratification and pleasure with no regard to the laws of God.

However, the Lord is merciful and kind. He will never ask you to do something that He does not first supply you with the ability to do. So come to Him in humbleness and simply ask Him to be your Saviour.

Although no one can tell us with certainly the exact timing of Jesus' return except our heavenly Father, I pray that after reading this book you are inspired to make your path straight before the Lord. If you feel somewhat backslidden, come before the Lord Jesus/Yeshua in true tears of repentance and receive His forgiveness (see 1 John 1:910).

We are not to avoid sharing about these signs of the end of the age. In fact, we read in Hebrews 10:2425,"And let us consider one another to provoke unto love and to good works: Not forsaking the assembling of ourselves together, as the manner of some is; but exhorting one another: and so much the more, as ye see the day approaching."

We ought to be meeting with each other regularly and encouraging each other as we see the day approaching.

Matthew 24:6-14, *"And ye shall hear of wars and rumours of wars: see that ye be not troubled: for all these things must come to pass, but the end is not yet. [7]For nation shall rise against nation, and kingdom against kingdom: and there shall be famines, and pestilences, and earthquakes, in divers places.[8]All these are the beginning of sorrows. [9]Then shall they deliver you up to be afflicted, and shall kill you: and ye shall be hated of all nations for my name's sake. [10]And then shall many be offended, and shall betray one another, and shall hate one another. [11]And many false prophets shall rise, and shall deceive many. [12]And because iniquity shall abound, the love of many shall wax cold. [13]But he that shall endure unto the end, the same shall be saved. [14]And this gospel of the kingdom shall be preached in all the world for a witness unto all nations; and then shall the end come."*

I do not want to stand before the Lord Jesus/Yeshua one day and try to explain why I kept these things to myself. What defense would I have to explain why I didn't help prepare people and help them draw closer to the Lord—that I was afraid of what they might think? That I didn't want them to think I was "fringe"?

We read of a time that will surely come when people will want to die and not be able to as told in Revelation 6:15-17:

"And the kings of the earth, and the great men, and the rich men, and the chief captains, and the mighty men, and every bondman, and every free man, hid themselves in the dens and in the rocks of the mountains; [16]And said to the mountains and rocks, Fall on us, and hide us from the face of him that sitteth on the throne, and from the wrath of the Lamb: [17]For the great day of his wrath is come; and who shall be able to stand?"

A day is coming when people will say to the mountains and rocks, "Fall on us," choosing death rather than life. Who will be able to stand in the day of the wrath of the Lord Jesus? He will be triumphant in that day, just as He was when He conquered death on the cross through His glorious resurrection.

What shall become of the Antichrist and his deranged sidekick, the false prophet? They shall be cast into the everlasting lake of fire after the Lord's millennium reign.

Revelation 19:20 *"And the beast was taken, and with him the false prophet that wrought miracles before him, with which he deceived them that had received the mark of the beast, and them that worshipped his image. These both were cast alive into a lake of fire burning with brimstone."*

For true believers, the story is quite different. We will join the Lord in the air, according to 1 Thessalonians 4: 16-17, *"For the Lord himself shall descend from heaven with a shout, with the voice of the archangel, and with the trump of God: and the dead in Christ shall rise first: Then we which are alive and remain shall be caught up together with them in the clouds, to meet the Lord in the air: and so shall we ever be with the Lord."*

I must also share that our Holy Guide Book to the Supernatural is filled with warnings. Before there was a universe and world here, Papa God already had a good plan for your life to be more than a conqueror through Christ's salvation and finished work on the cross. The Lord did not save you and then wonder, "What in the world am I going to do with this person now?" AU CONTRAIRE!

The Lord Jesus saved you because He truly loves you. In fact, you were created for His pleasure according to Revelation 4:11, *"Thou art worthy, O Lord, to receive glory and honour and power: for thou hast created all things, and for thy pleasure they are and were created."*

The Lord has a divine purpose for you in the grand scheme of things, even if you don't understand it all this side of heaven. There is simply no such thing as an insignificant person. When you surrender to the Lord, know that He already has a plan and will equip you to do what is necessary. There is no point in ever running like Jonah did to be swallowed by a whale and then still live to give the message the Lord said to give in the first place. Remember, it is God who will accomplish the assignment through you.

Philippians 2:13 *"For it is God which worketh in you both to will and to do of his good pleasure."*

There are a number of places in which we are assured that Jesus Christ of Nazareth/Messiah Yeshua—the eternal, living Lord of all creation—shall return to this Earth and there will be NO mistaking Him when this occurs. It is written that EVERY EYE shall see Him. The troubles in this world today appear insurmountable, however all things are possible with God and He has provided the way for us to overcome the world through Christ. The apostle Paul endured many things, but the Lord delivered him out of all of them. And He will do the same for us.

2 Timothy 3:11 *"Persecutions, afflictions, which came unto me at Antioch, at Iconium, at Lystra; what persecutions I endured: but out of them all the Lord delivered me."*

No matter what we may go through, we should comfort one another with the truth that all believers will also be given glorified, indestructible, immortal bodies and we will be with the Lord Jesus forever!

A Prayer of Salvation

If you desire the Lord Jesus to save you and preserve you and provide a place for you in heaven, you may wish to pray this prayer:

"Dear God in Heaven, I recognise that I need a Savior, who is Jesus Christ. I ask You to please forgive me of all my sins and fill me with Your Holy Spirit. Your Word says that if I confess with my mouth that Jesus is Lord, and believe in my heart that God raised Him from the dead, I will be saved (Romans 10:9). So Lord I believe with all my heart and I confess with my mouth that Jesus is now the Lord and Saviour of my life and I want to live a life that is glorifying to Him.

I truly believe that Jesus died in my place as payment for all my sins, and that He rose again defeating the power of sin and death that I might be saved and born again. Because You are so merciful to forgive me and wash me clean from all unrighteousness, I choose to also forgive from my heart, all those who have done wrong to me, including myself.

Thank You for saving me, I am so eternally grateful for what you have done for me! I pray this in Jesus' name. Amen."

By making this confession, you are now a child of the Lord your God! Please share your decision with me, I would love to hear about it. You can send me an email or share your testimony at: pastorcaspar@gmail.com or www.theupperroomfellowship.org

A Prayer for Yourself

This prayer is for anyone who, in reading these pages, has had their conscience pricked by the Holy Spirit and you want to be clean before the Lord. Pray this out loud so both invisible kingdoms hear you:

"Papa God, in the name of Jesus Christ of Nazareth, I speak Your promise that no weapon formed against me shall prosper. That includes any heretical teaching, and words spoken or prayed against me. I forgive anyone who has sought to do me harm and all those who have abandoned and rejected me.

Having forgiven them I also confess any sin on my part towards them and I bless them in the name of Jesus.

I declare, O Lord, that You and You alone are my God, and besides You there is no other. I worship You Father, Jesus my Saviour, and the Holy Ghost.

I submit myself to You today in unreserved obedience and do as Your Word directs me. I choose to resist the devil and all his pressure to cause me to submit to an evil spirit of fear, or any other unclean thing. I resist all his deceptions and everything he tries to use against me. I will not submit to the devil, but rather resist him so he will flee. I exclude him in the almighty name of Jesus.

I reject all false teaching from outside and inside the Church. I command all unclean spirits to leave me, including spirits of infirmity, infections, inflammations, malignancies, allergies, and all spirits of viruses. I command all spirits of pain to leave my body now, in Jesus' name.

I commit my life to You so that anything coming on this planet will not alarm me or cause me to fear or doubt Your power. I commit to staying in faith. From what I'm reading in this book, I am being made aware of the end times and I will no longer keep my head in the sand, but be aware, watching and praying even though many others fall away. I pray you will keep me strong in the truth. I reject every form of witchcraft and manipulation coming from the enemy in these last days, and command those spirits of torment to leave me, in Jesus' name.

Thank You Papa God that through the ultimate sacrifice of Jesus Christ of Nazareth on the cross, I have escaped the curse and can enter into the blessings of Father Abraham, whom You blessed in all things. Thank You for the gifts of health, prosperity, and victory in Jesus.

A Prayer for Others

"Papa God, as one of your representatives, I ask that You bless your people. I command in the almighty name of Jesus that every tormenting spirit be bound and their assignments be cancelled now. Reveal any sin that needs to brought before Your throne of grace. I thank you for your mercy and grace upon our lives that cleanses us from all sin.

I pray the blind eyes be open, the deaf hear, and the lame get up and walk. I pray that cancer and diseases vanish out of Your people's bodies. I pray the blessings of Abraham overtake them in the all powerful name of Jesus Christ of Nazareth, Messiah/Yeshua. To You be all the Glory!"

Hallelujah! Amen!

PROPHECY WATCHERS
August 2016

We were delighted to have Caspar McCloud join us in Colorado Springs and grace us with his musical talents. Rumour has it that he even made up a song about L.A. Marzulli on the spot. Caspar is pictured here with (L-R) Trey Smith and Joe Ardis Horn (Tom Horn's son) and Bob Ulrich in the background

Caspar McCloud worshipping and praising God all throughout the **Prophesy Watchers** conference!

FURTHER GROWTH

Caspar McCloud Books & Music available on Amazon and iTunes and at www.theupperroomfellowship.org

- Nothing Is Impossible by Caspar McCloud (updated and revised)
- What Was I Thinking? by Caspar McCloud coauthored with Linda Lange of Life Application Ministries. Updated and revised May 31, 2015.
- Exposing the Spirit of Self-Pity by Caspar McCloud
- The Evidence of the Shroud Speaks for Itself by Simon Brown and Caspar McCloud
- Spiritual Encounters With The Shroud, Caspar McCloud interviewed by L. A. Marzulli

CONTACT US

Pastor Caspar McCloud
Upper Room Fellowship c/o
Freedom's Light Church of God
175 Marion Spence Road
Ball Ground, Georgia 30107

casparmccloudmusic.com
pastorcaspar@gmail.com
www.theupperroomfellowship.org
NonProfit 501c3

James - 12-3

51257202R00094

Made in the USA
San Bernardino, CA
19 July 2017